P9-DMB-134

FINGER LICKIN' GOOD

By the same author

(Ed.) Lytton Strachey: The Really Interesting Question
Moore: G. E. Moore and the Cambridge Apostles
(With Ann Barr) The Official Foodie Handbook
(Ed., with Michael Holroyd) The Shorter Strachey
Out to Lunch

Finger Lickin' Good

A KENTUCKY CHILDHOOD

Paul Levy

Chatto & Windus
LONDON

TO ALISTAIR MCALPINE

Published in 1990 by
Chatto & Windus Ltd
20 Vauxhall Bridge Road
London SW1V 2SA

All rights reserved. No part of this publication may be
reproduced, stored in a retrieval system, or transmitted in any form,
or by any means, electronic, mechanical, photocopying,
recording or otherwise, without the prior permission
of the publisher.

A CIP Catalogue record for this book is available from the
British Library

ISBN 0 7011 3521 2

Copyright © Paul Levy 1990

Paul Levy has asserted his right to be
identified as the author of this work

Typeset at The Spartan Press Ltd,
Lymington, Hants
Printed in Great Britain by
Mackays of Chatham plc,
Chatham, Kent

Contents

Great-grandfather Chaim Singer,
the sacred scribe, with two of his
descendants, the author and
cousin Paul.

Introduction

This is, of course, a work of fiction. The human memory is a poor thing, and my own seems to be getting feeble much sooner than it should. So, when trying to recall the events and sensations of a childhood forty-odd years ago, I am at a disadvantage. In my view there is no point in a narration such as this unless it is both funny and truthful. But when remembering our childhoods, we can only be certain that we now think it was like that then – or that that is the way we should have liked it to be. I hope everything that follows is true; I mean it to be.

How does one deal with the inevitability that some people are bound to be wounded – or at least annoyed – by an autobiography? The living mind so terribly much what is said about the dead, especially about the recently dead. One can only take refuge in truthfulness; or, rather, one's hope that candour and truth coincide. In any case, my mother's worst fears are baseless; this book is not, as she was alarmed it would be when she learnt I was writing about my early memories, '*Mommy Dearest* with recipes'.

There is no excuse for writing about yourself unless what you have to say is either amusing or edifying. No one will be edified by anything that has happened to me, but I think some people will find some of this entertaining. Childhood *is* another country; and mine was *in* another country. I've lived in England, off and on, since my early twenties – more than half my life. People say I sound English, and to some extent, I think like an Englishman. Certainly the cadences of the British version of our common language come more naturally to me than those I was born to listen to and to speak.

But it's all an accident. Inside this apparent Brit, there's a sceptical American kid struggling to get out – or at least to make himself heard through the Oxbridge accent. I was born in America, in one of the southern states (at least, *we* thought Kentucky was in the south; those who live there still do, though non-natives are inclined to think of it as a border state), the grandchild of (I believe) four Russian Jews. It didn't seem out of the ordinary to me at first, though even as a child there were clues I should have perceived that we were not as others. It wasn't, however, until I moved to England and had children of my own, that I was able to see the essential foreign-ness of my own childhood. Because I've ended up as a journalist, I've travelled a lot. While everybody recognises the essential truth of Thomas Wolfe's claim that you can't go home again, the corollary of this in my life is that no matter where I am, I'm permanently abroad. In an agreeable sense, there's no place where I am not a foreigner. So when I look back on my old Kentucky home, I have a distinctly Martian's-eye view: it all seems very odd.

Chapter One

In my dreams I often return to my grandparents' house. I don't know why, as I don't think I was particularly happy there – or unhappy either. But after our parents were divorced, my father went back and lived there for a time; so we children were very often in the house as well. At least every Sunday, the day our father had charge of us, and, of course, on the principal Jewish holidays, when I, as the elder son, was invariably forced to go to the synagogue with my father. Maybe I think about the house, or dream about it because it's something rooted and comforting in my subsequent near-vagabond life. It's possible, however, that my subconscious mind keeps going back to Kalmia Road, Lexington, Kentucky, simply because it was so interesting.

Lexington is now the world centre of the Thoroughbred horse breeding industry and trade. The Queen has twice gone there on holiday and keeps a mare or two there. When I was born in February, 1941, it was a sleepy southern college town with a population of about 45,000, and my paternal grand-father, Joe Levy, owned, or had owned, a great deal of the county in which it was situated. The city is now a vigorous, urbane place of 250,000 sophisticated souls, of whom quite a few are millionaires – some of them Arab princelings with oil money. The surrounding farmland is amongst the most valu-able acreage on earth. My grandfather gave a lot of it away, mostly to brothers-in-law, I have heard, whom he endowed with a parcel of land as a welcoming present when he brought them over, one by one, from Russia. When he died, Joe Levy left about 350 acres of prime Bluegrass country. He had never learnt English properly, he never lived on his land, and as soon as he made enough money, he bought a shop in order to be respectable. What on earth was he doing there?

Ethnically, my grandfather considered himself a *Litvak*, a Lithuanian Jew. This manifested itself chiefly – even exclusively – in his contempt for Jews of Polish and German origin. In reality, this was more a case of prejudices than a clue to his own geographical origins. On his American citizenship documents, his former nationality is given as German. Much though it would have distressed him to know that I am making this public, it might well help to establish the whereabouts of Pushelot (can this be the correct spelling? I have never seen the word written), the village or *shtetl* from whence he came. Even my parents' generation found the idea, or at least the sound of the word, Pushelot, comic, and joked that it must have been the twin town of Camelot. Though a great many of the 500 or so Jewish families of Lexington in my time seem also to have had forbears from Pushelot, I never met anybody with the slightest notion of where it actually was.

But if the American authorities regarded my grandfather as a German, it is likely that he came from a fairly small area on the Baltic near the Lithuanian–Polish border, where the principal cities have German names that are still more familiar to us than their Slavic ones. Danzig is more meaningful to me than Gdansk, and I rather hope that, like Immanuel Kant, my grandparent emanated from Königsberg, which I have never learnt to call Kaliningrad. The rulers of this stretch of the Baltic coast changed frequently – even regularly – and perhaps it was German territory when my grandfather left it.

Unfortunately, I don't know exactly when that was, except that it was sometime around the turn of the century. He was always said to have left for the usual reason, to avoid conscription into the Tsar's army. On the other hand, he told me that he *had* been a soldier, though only a boy, in the drum and bugle corps – not that he ever showed any evidence of musical gifts – where he played what he called the 'fife'. So perhaps he was a deserter from the Tsar's forces, a common enough reason for Jews to flee Russia in the early twentieth century. Of course, both these speculations clash with the theory that he was German in nationality. I have an idea at the back of my mind that he once told me that his departure from Russia was connected with the abortive revolution of 1905. But then, the only time I ever really talked with my grandfather was when he was very old – in his late seventies or even eighty – and I was an undergraduate with left-wing leanings. He was sick, perhaps a little senile, and given to small romances such as that he had known Lenin, who was in reality of good Jewish family, and who ought, therefore, to have known better than to go around making trouble. Once or twice my grandfather confided in me that he had personally told Lenin that his time would be better spent in the synagogue than in revolutionary meetings.

None of this, however, explains what Joe Levy was doing in Lexington. In the first place, that wasn't his real name; it was a *nom d'émigration* bestowed upon him by a US immigration official at his port of entry. His real surname, transliterated from the Russian, I presume, was Lygon. (I am sorry he died before I discovered and could have told him that that is also the family name of the former Earls of Beauchamp; he would almost certainly have regarded it as evidence of their apostasy – like Lenin's.) As for his given name, I don't ever remember my grandparents addressing each other in the vocative, so I don't know if he was Yusef or Yussel to my grandmother; to his grandchildren he was Zedeh, a word I had trouble getting my tongue around and never thought to ask how to spell. To most of the world, though, he was just plain Joe.

The surname is easy to explain. Grandfather spoke no English when he entered America through one of the Gulf ports. Yiddish must have been his mother tongue, though he must have known some Hebrew. Rena Niles, the Russian-born widow of the folk singer John Jacob Niles, told me she used to depend on my grandfather for occasional Russian conversation, so that must be added to his language store as well. But upon his arrival in America, we must imagine that he could not communicate readily with the southerner representing the US Immigration Service, who was doubtless at least a tiny bit anti-Semitic. Faced with an obvious but nameless Jew, he followed what was standard practice and re-baptised my grandfather with one of the two aristocratic Jewish names.

It must have been very satisfactory to create so many Levys and Cohens: it not only devalued the currency to hand out these grandest of names wholesale, but had the added merit of branding indelibly their bearers as Jews. A later refinement was to give the name Rothschild to the Jewish fraction of the tired, the poor and the huddled masses yearning to breathe free. My grandmother's family, of Kavarsk, Lithuania, acquired their surname in a related fashion. Her Russian name was simple, Barron or Baron (there are still cousins called that, though I have yet to meet them). One of her brothers was, for some unaccountable reason, heading for a town in Tennessee called Herman or Hermann – his sole lexical item of English. The unlovely Herman thus became her American family name.

Perhaps her family had already got to America and Tennessee; that would account for my grandfather's coming up from the south, rather than entering the States in the orthodox way, through New York. Family mythology says he began his new life as an itinerant pedlar of dry goods. The trouble with that is that I have scarcely heard of any well-off southern Jewish family whose founder did *not* start off as an itinerant pedlar; and it seems to me inconceivable that anybody could sell sufficient quantities of bootlaces and sealing-wax to amass enough capital to buy the quantity of land Joe Levy once owned.

I know, however, how he got rich once he owned the farms. In the opening years of the First World War – most probably in 1915 – the US Government, desperately worried about a shortage of rope for the navy, paid a huge price to farmers who would agree to grow hemp, a particularly nasty crop to harvest. My grandfather agreed, but only on condition that he was given a contract to grow hemp for the duration of the war – and at the same high price. The remnants of that crop can still be found on the farms, growing under the fences and in the hedgerows. I know, because hemp is *Cannabis indica*, and in the flower-power sixties a houseparty of Harvard and Oxford friends discovered it and smoked a great deal of it to no avail.

Why did Joe Levy even *want* to own land? It remains a mystery to me. Where he had come from, Jews were not only forbidden to own land, but were the eternal enemies of those who farmed. The *shtetl* may have been in the countryside, but the Jewish village was itself most definitely not rural. Rural people were not Jews; they were landowners or peasants, and in either case, makers of pogroms. This no doubt accounts for my grandfather never wishing actually to live on his own land: it does not explain his wishing to own it in the first place. There were other Jewish farmers in Lexington but, so far as I can remember, they were all German Jews, despised by my grandfather for their presumed snobbery and unorthodox religious views, and sheep farmers to boot. Grandfather was a cattleman. He also grew tobacco, a special kind, called Burley, which makes the light strands you can see in any Virginia cigarette. It is not particularly aromatic, but it is slow-burning and keeps the other tobaccos in the blend from going up in a whoosh of flames.

I don't really believe my grandfather was ever a tiller of the soil. We always had a tenant farmer called Fred Baesler, who must have begun with my grandfather as a young boy. Fred did all the work and, in recent years at least, received fifty per cent of the profits. I used to hate the farms, and was a bit embarrassed about the family ownership of them. One reason was that I associated them with muck and dirt (and certainly they were never so tidy in my grandfather's day as they are now). Another was that, as a young boy, I was made to accompany my grandfather to visit them on Sunday. How could my parents have allowed it?

Here was I, the elder son of my grandfather's only son, the heir presumptive, and, I never doubted, my parents' favoured child, seated in the passenger position of a pick-up truck, driven by my grandfather, who must surely have been legally blind. I think it was cataracts that affected the old man's eyes – this was in the days before the removal of them from quite elderly people had become the routine operation it now is. The farms were all located on the Athens (pronounced Ay-thens) to Boonesborough road, which you reached by heading out on the Richmond Road, then as now a main thorough-fare. How did my grandfather negotiate this busy road, Sunday after Sunday? Why did we never run into the on-coming traffic? Why did we never see another car? How did Grandfather even manage to keep the pick-up truck on his own side of the road?

We shall never know the answer to these questions. But I think I owe my survival to the local constabulary. After all, Grandfather's routine never varied. We left the house on Kalmia Road at precisely the same time each Sunday, in the pick-up, and drove by exactly the same route. The Athens–Boonesborough part was easy: the police simply closed the road to all other traffic until Joe Levy and his terrified grandson were on their own property. I don't ever remember meeting another car at all though. Perhaps the reason was that the route took us through Bible Belt country, so deeply evangelical Christian that, at that time on Sunday morning, every potential driver of another car was in church.

It's a pity I knew so little of my grandfather's character. As a child I suspected him of eccentricity. Whether I would have liked it if he had turned out to be odd, I cannot say. I, of course, craved conformity. The very existence of my grandfather made us different. The child snob in me detested his shop. It was called Levy and Herman – I suppose the Herman partner or partners were brothers of my grandmother (of whom I remember two with affection) – and it sold workmen's and farmers' clothes and uniforms for domestic servants. It had a stale, dusty smell about it. It was in downtown Lexington, a few doors up from Joe Rosenberg's pawn shop, a place of real interest, with glass display cases packed with unredeemed or second-hand banjos, guitars and complicated mouth organs.

My grandparents' house was kosher, or what passed for it in Kentucky. I do not think my grandfather was seriously religious. Certainly he used to preside over the Passover Seder ceremony, he always the eldest man, I the perpetual youngest boy (my younger brother never counted for ritual purposes). Part of our family rites consisted in hiding a bit of the special matzoth, the Passover unleavened bread. I think this portion was called the *aphikomen*, and I think if I could spell it properly it would resemble the Greek word for dessert. I became so efficient at disguising the whereabouts of this essential bit of the feast, that my grandfather used, cynically I thought, to bribe me to reveal its hiding place without making any real effort to look for it. I also remember vividly the part of the proceedings that describe the ten plagues divinely visited upon the Egyptians. As he named each one – boils, plague, pestilence – Grandfather would dip the wrong end of a spoon into his wineglass, and use it to spill exactly one drop of wine on to his plate. It reminded me of blood. I think it did him, too. He obviously relished imagining the horrors of these plagues: it was the late forties, and the Egyptians he had in mind spoke German.

Grandfather went to synagogue often enough, and participated in the tuneless anarchy that has always seemed to me to characterise Orthodox Jewish divine worship. In fact, the location of his house was chosen for its proximity to the synagogue. It was an easy walk. Too easy, if anyone had asked me. I hated going to the synagogue. But it was hopeless to seek escape from at least occasional attendance; for the synagogue was my grandmother's special province. She was always credited with founding the religious school attached to it. I think the truth was more likely that, hiding behind my grandfather's trousers, she was one of the founders of the synagogue herself.

I scarcely knew or remember my grandmother — to the extent that I don't really know what her English given name was. But then, I don't suppose anyone ever used it. I think all her children — and I know all her friends — could speak Yiddish. Her name was either Mary or Jenny; though the latter is a little unlikely, as that was the name of her eldest child, and Jewish custom does not allow children to bear the names of living relations. In Yiddish she was called Yachne or Yetta — perhaps her Hebrew name was Mary. To me she was, of course, *bubba*, another word that our southern drawl found difficult to manage. I can remember blushing with shame as a sophisticated Jewish kid from the north — which might have been Cleveland or Cincinnati as easily as New York — teased me for my pronunciation of the universal Jewish child's name for his grandmother. My brother and I were quick and careful to find a circumlocution for use in public. Until her death, to me my grandmother was only a domestic personality, one whose indifferent and bland cooking (except for dishes dangerous to health that involved large quantities of onion-flavoured, rendered chicken fat) it was obligatory to praise. Little hypocrites all, we duly praised it, while always hoping to avoid it in favour of a non-kosher hamburger.

My grandmother's existence, too, was the reason I had to be *bar mitzvah*. This was torture, and I am unhappy to say I was not let off even though she died before my thirteenth birthday. My father and grandfather made me go through with it for the sake of her memory. When she died, Harry Goller, the local kosher butcher and purveyor of Jewish gastronomic necessities such as smoked salmon, who was a relation of hers by marriage, delivered a half-hour long eulogy in Yiddish – in the synagogue of course. It was histrionic; it was hysterical. It involved screaming and weeping and hooting with laughter. The Reverend Mr Goller (for he had some claim to clerical status) was by turns a manic Othello and a depressed Hamlet – and that was between his renditions of a raving King Lear and Macbeth in a 'I-have-lived-long-enough' mood. I understood not a word of it. I was moved, though: I was terror-struck.

The burial could not take place in Lexington. In his idiosyncratic version of English, Mr Goller, with whom I was made to sit in the lead limousine of the long funeral entourage, explained to me why we were driving ninety miles to Louisville to bury my grandmother. It seems there was no ground in Lexington sacred enough to receive her remains. In Louisville there was a Jewish cemetery, and there was a corner of this cemetery reserved for those who had kept the Sabbath and otherwise scrupulously observed the letter of the Jewish law. Only God's little acre would do for my grandmother, said Mr Goller. That was how I learnt that Grandmother was a Jewish saint.

From her plot in Louisville, Grandmother, said Mr Goller, simplifying for the juvenile mind and falsifying the five thousand years of Jewish theology that has denied the existence of an afterlife, went straight to heaven. (I am pleased to think that Grandfather, who was emphatically *not* a Sabbath-observer in the intended sense, got to heaven on her coat tails; for the plot was a double one, and when his turn came nobody raised any objection to his occupying this privileged spot.)

Grandmother, I learnt much later, was very well qualified for sainthood. I realised on her death that she had been an educated woman. I was old enough to go through the bookshelves that, I had not known until then, contained her personal library. The books (which I should have given a great deal to have had, but which were dispersed without anybody asking me) were in five or six languages, and those in Cyrillic type were, I now believe, editions of the Russian classics. Unusual though it was for a girl to be educated, she was so clever (said her brother, my great-uncle Nathan Herman) that their rabbinical father, Yechiel Asher Baron, allowed her to be schooled with the boys. This would explain her literacy in Hebrew, and her acquaintance with religious learning, and why Mr Goller and the others considered her an authority on Talmudic matters and such like. It doesn't explain her other languages or any of her secular education. And I don't think it explains why her house on Kalmia Road in Lexington, Kentucky, was once – I think – visited by Rabbi Kook, the first Ashkenazi Chief Rabbi of what was then Palestine, and any other notable passing through the southern United States.

The actual reason was that she was related to Rabbi Kook. I have never been able to learn the exact connection – but a connection there certainly was. If proof be needed, there was the occasion of a visit to Kook's yeshiva by my father and me (most unwillingly, as I was hot in pursuit of yet another of my collection of left-wing kibbutzim) in 1962, when we were received as Founder's Kin (and, I churlishly remarked to my father, prayed to by the young devotees).

I don't know why none of this emerged in my grandmother's lifetime. Unfortunately, I wasn't interested. I'm sure she would have answered my questions with a good grace – if I'd asked any. Her own children, then good Americans all, were not of a generation that wanted to be reminded of the immigrant past: they were just too busy making a success of the present.

But there you are. My grandmother possessed, and no doubt carried in her head, the details of what Jews call the unbroken line, a pedigree that goes back to the House of David. Sir Ian Moncrieffe of that ilk, the greatest (and funniest) genealogist of our age, explained to me, in the back of a London taxi before we began an all-day drinking session which took in eleven London clubs, that it was the second oldest pedigree in the world. (The descendents of Confucius can claim the record.) My grandmother, had she wished (which she certainly didn't), could have called Jesus cousin.

Somewhere, lost amongst the thousands of books in my crumbling seventeenth-century Oxfordshire farm house is an entire book dealing with my grandmother's pedigree. I can, however, find a long essay [see Appendix] I wrote myself several years ago, following a week's research at the Widener Library of Harvard, done to amuse myself while my wife bullied an elderly Harvard professor into producing the manuscript of his much-delayed book on ancient Chinese painting. There is also another family tree, showing the more recent connections of the family, prepared by a cousin from Baltimore whom I have never met.

Fortunately, Rabbi Kook was important enough to rate an entry in a massive one-volume encyclopaedia that I *am* able to find. So I can say that his name was Abraham Isaac, that he was born in Latvia in 1864 and died, revered by Jew and Arab alike (for he favoured a bi-national policy), in Palestine in 1935. The *Columbia Encyclopaedia* calls him a philosopher as well as a scholar. He moved to Palestine in 1904 and became Ashkenazi Chief Rabbi in 1921. One of his distinctions was that he applied his reading of the Talmud to the problems of the day, which led him to the conclusion that the non-religious Zionist Jews were unwittingly doing God's work, as would be evident to them one day. He seems to have held an almost Marxist belief that nationalism was a necessary historical stage to a universalist withering away of the state.

Though I seem to have met his daughter and son-in-law in 1962, Rov Kook's beliefs and deeds are of less interest to me than his genealogy; he was descended from a rabbinical line that could trace itself back to Rashi, whose dates were 1040–1105. There was a little trouble about whether some seventeenth-century documents were genuine or forgeries, but apart from that the pedigree chart flows smoothly back to the great Jewish exegete, grammarian and legal scholar born in Troyes. (I have more than once looked for traces of him there; most recently Jane Grigson and I failed to get past the French security police at the synagogue on a Saturday morning; it was shortly after the bombing of Jo Goldenberg's, the Jewish deli on the rue du Rosier in Paris, and I do not think I could have convinced the gendarme on duty of the purity of my motives in wanting to assist in the offices.)

I do hope I am descended from Rashi – the name is an acronym for Rabbi Solomon bar Isaac – because it would mean that champagne flows in my blood. After studying in Worms, he came back to Troyes about 1065 – a year before the Conquest – and, the part I like best, supported himself on the income from the family vineyards. Rashi was, naturally, descended from the house of David. This makes my family eligible for the most exalted office of both this world and the next, if you're a believer. The romance of the unbroken line.

Though I always understood that it was Joe Levy who built the house on Kalmia Road, it was not architecturally negligible but an adaptation of a typical, small town American house to southern requirements. I doubt whether my grandfather could have got together the money to build the house much before the 1914–18 war, and in any case Lexington always was and remains a step or two behind the fashions. Though it was in the

14

architectural vernacular, the design of the house was therefore gracious and Edwardian. It was, I think, faced with local limestone.

My grandparents' first house had been on Upper Street, now smack in the centre of the downtown. Several of the houses on Upper Street are tiny eighteenth-century, Federal period, wooden-frame townhouses, now much prized but, naturally, despised by my grandparents' generation. It has to be counted good luck that any of them have survived, so unloved were they until very recently. Their front doors give straight on to the pavement, and my recollection is that few of the houses on Upper Street had any front garden, but most had a few steps up from the pavement to the front porch (an essential architectural feature of every southern house), in the centre of which was the front door. Perhaps because the houses were built on small plots of land with small gardens or none at all, Upper Street was not a socially desirable address. (I remember one of my aunts saying cattily, and perhaps inaccurately, about the parents of a now celebrated American writer, 'Oh yes, I remember them. They were still living on Upper Street long after we left.')

So Joe Levy's new house had a strip of lawn, through the centre of which ran a sidewalk, perpendicular to the pavement, leading up to the steps to the front porch. This was capacious enough to house several large pieces of outdoor furniture, including a swing the size of a small sofa. It was unenclosed, and depended on some scrubby shrubs to give the porch a little privacy from the neighbours on either side. You entered into the living room – which they may have called the parlour – with its overstuffed Edwardian furniture draped with antimacassars, wax-polished bare hardwood floors, and a thrilling gas log fire in the fireplace that, in fact, supplemented a central heating system that blew hot air through interestingly ornate metal grilles placed in the floor. The living room was large. To the right of the front door was a room of which I don't remember the name, entered from the parlour and separated from it by a set of open shelves on the left of the doorway. This room contained a pair of armchairs and a settee, a glass-fronted bookcase holding what I learnt after her death were my grandmother's books, and a piano that got progressively more out of tune as I got older. Its hinged seat contained stacks of sheet music for popular songs of the twenties and thirties; I taught myself to pick out their melodies in the treble. But it was no use: there was no way to compensate for the unmusicality of the instrument itself. This room also contained the one ornament that seems central to every childhood that has ever been memorialised in print – a sphere which, inverted, contains an internal snowstorm. (It makes the grown-up me giggle, because it reminds me of Hans Castorp's epiphany in *Magic Mountain* – a book I actually love – and so satisfactorily trivialises its hero's pomposity.)

You walked through the living room or parlour into the dining room with its massive mahogany table and chairs that seated the whole disparate clan of my aunts, uncles and first cousins, who numbered more than a dozen. The sideboard held small prayer books containing the interminably tedious grace after meals that made the Sabbath as great a torture as the proper holidays; a supply of skullcaps for the men and boys; a biscuit tin with delicious cookies baked by my youngest aunt – so far as I know, her sole culinary accomplishment; and a decanter of Bourbon whiskey, into which my grandfather used to place bruised cherrystones, in the belief that this made a tipple of great potency. They certainly made the Bourbon taste good; I suppose he was attempting to re-create one of the cherry *eaux-de-vie* of eastern Europe; *Kirschwasser* was not something we saw much of in Lexington.

A screened-in verandah went the length of the back of the house, from the dining room through to the kitchen. Internally you reached the kitchen via the pantry with its floor-to-ceiling cupboards, so necessary to a kosher *ménage*, which was obliged to find storage space for two of everything. In fact, my grandmother kept four of everything, as the Passover requires its own two sets of cutlery, crockery, glasses and pots and pans. I never got the hang of keeping the meat things separate from the dairy utensils, and in consequence was never required to help with the washing up. Mind you, this household, though a strictly kosher matriarchy, shared totally the assumptions of any male chauvinist pig. In any case, as the son of my mother, I could not be trusted to keep the forks segregated.

The kitchen ought to be the heart of the Jewish home, and it ought to be at least as clean as an operating theatre. My grandmother's kitchen was, to my eyes, squalid. The kitchen range and sink alike could not be called antique only because that word seems to me to convey some sort of aesthetic praise. They were old and filthy with stains, the result of heating both chicken fat and cooking oil to high temperatures and of cleaning the cooking vessels with wire wool pads and foul-smelling kosher soap. There was a larder, really a walk-in cupboard off the kitchen, containing the Ur-refrigerator that had replaced the icebox even in my own lifetime, and shelves of jars containing unattractive things. For some reason, this cupboard also housed the tin collecting boxes for the Jewish charities. Pride of place on the grimy shelf was given to the one for Rabbi Kook's yeshiva. There was a kitchen table and chairs that belonged in a cheap diner, off which my father would feed us his bachelor dinners of kosher hot dogs or too thinly sliced corned beef (salt beef in British Yinglish) procured by calling on Mr Goller at precisely the right time on Sunday morning.

We southern, small town Jews felt keenly the deprivation of the Jewish gastronomic birthright, and were capable of behaving badly to our fellow Jews, and even of resorting to complicated subterfuge, to cheat them of the last morsel of Mr Goller's smoked salmon (which, until the age of twenty-one, when I first saw on a London table an entire side of smoked salmon, I had thought came exclusively in tins) or halvah. I never knew how or where Mr Goller got his minuscule supplies of these golden goods. Perhaps they fell off the back of the lorry conveying them to the proper Jewish delicatessens of the metropolises of Louisville or Cincinnati, both about ninety miles distant from Lexington. Maybe there was some Jewish version of the underground railroad that went through Lexington in the 1860s taking slaves to the north and freedom, now working in reverse to bring us bagels. My father's favourite supper dish – quite likely the only one he knew how to make – was fried squares of garlicky kosher salami with egg scrambled in chicken fat; a triumph of cholesterol, and very good. My mother used to wonder how we could bear to eat it, or anything else, in that kitchen. She had a point.

The back door of the kitchen led, to the left, to the verandah, which was never used except to store garden furniture, which was also never used. No wonder. If you turned right, a dangerously rickety wooden staircase lurched down to the dustbowl that was once the back garden. There was little need to mow the lawn; the grass was as exhausted as the fruit trees that struggled to exist at the bottom of the lawn. A near-by garage housed what I have just convinced myself was the pick-up truck. This bit of scrubland was overlooked on the first floor by the most attractive feature of the house, which was called the sleeping porch. It was completely open but screened in on three sides, and my brother and I were allowed to sleep there on hot nights. It was usually cool. Otherwise, memory tells me that there were four large bedrooms on the first floor, and one bathroom with old-fashioned plumbing of a type that now only exists at the Savoy Hotel. This was the only bathroom. Otherwise there was the smelliest lavatory I have encountered outside China, situated near the stairs on the ground floor, and positioned so that it had to be passed on the way to the kitchen. The noises that came from it were as pungent as the smells and it flushed with the roar of a waterfall powerful enough to have run an electricity generator.

The second floor was, I think, entirely attics. But that is the bit that I find fascinating when I revisit in my dreams. I can never get much beyond the staircase in reverie. In memory I can recall finding an old wind-up gramophone with a packet of steel needles in the attic; but I cannot remember the configuration of rooms. There ought to have been a bedroom or two upstairs, for there must once have been four children living in the house. But no servants. Any normal Lexington family as well off and substantially housed as my grandparents would have had a maid or two, or at the very least what Grandmother would have called a *schwartze* to clean. Surprisingly, I don't ever remember even a black maid in the house. On the other hand, I don't suppose Orthodox Jews could really employ a servant who wasn't of the same persuasion, and though there were some relatively poor Jews in Lexington, I don't suppose there were any of a social status low enough to do domestic work. And in any case, I imagine my grandmother's life was bound up with doing the housework herself, not just to avoid ritual pollution, but because she was psychologically the servant of her husband and children.

The children, besides my father, were my three aunts. The eldest, Jenny, was born in Europe, which proves that my grandparents were married before they emigrated. Jenny was always supposed to have a good heart, and I was and am very fond of her children, ten-years older than me, Marvin, a successful, Harvard-trained Cincinnati lawyer who, along with his sister Ruth (and my younger brother), are the only ones of my paternal first cousins who don't have Ph.D.s. Jenny had a piercing, corncrake's voice, and she chattered constantly. When she got old, I think she came to disapprove of me. Rebecca, the second daughter, and Esther, the fourth and youngest child, had university educations as did my father. This was extremely unusual for southern girls, let alone Jewish ones, and must have been my grandmother's doing. It was, after all, only the secular equivalent of the education she had received. Aunt Beck, who was always frankly plump in the time I knew her, was supposed to be the best cook in the family. She had studied social work at the University of Chicago under the great Jane Addams, the Nobel Prize winner who founded the pernicious discipline. I don't know if Aunt Beck ever practised. She married, in Chicago, and I mostly remember her and Uncle Nathan running a pathetic men's and boys' clothing shop in the near-by one-horse town of Winchester, where my father bought all my clothes, ensuring that I was usually badly dressed. Nathan became prematurely senile, until some clever doctor spotted that there was something wrong with his medication. Whereupon, aged sixty, he became positively agile mentally and began taking a university degree. Esther married badly, a Jewish bounder from Michigan, I think. My brother and I loathed him from infancy and, as soon as we knew the word, called him Uncle Fuck, which rhymed with the diminutive by which he was generally known. Esther divorced him in great style. She gave the only grand party I ever knew her to give, on a Sunday night at a local country club, with generous food and drink. The next morning, Uncle Fuck read in the Monday paper, as did the rest of us, that it had been his farewell party: Aunt Esther had filed divorce proceedings on Friday. His crime was that he had got a local country girl pregnant. He'd been having an affair with her for years, it seems. But she soon kicked him out, and he got into fairly heavy money troubles. When last seen, he was seeking protection from the law's long arm, trying to emigrate to Israel, a confessed petty criminal invoking the Law of Return.

The proximity of the grandparental house to the synagogue meant that on days of compulsory attendance, such as the High Holy Days of Rosh Hashanah and Yom Kippur, we children were allowed some time off. On the Day of Atonement, we were only expected to go without breakfast, not to observe a full fast, and we were allowed to break the fast at the lunch counter of Dunn's drugstore. The menu there featured such southern delicacies as olive-nut and pimiento cheese sandwiches. These were concoctions made gooey with mayonnaise, the first consisting of stuffed green olives, chopped together with walnuts or pecans, the second of a fairly sharp cheddar-type cheese, combined with bottled sweet red peppers, and, if the lunch counter was sophisticated, a pinch of cayenne or a drop of Tabasco. With crisp lettuce on fresh toast, these were irresistable.

Except on Yom Kippur, when my brother and I always made a point of ordering a ham sandwich. The particular thrill of it was the chance that some pious member of the congregation might have need of the chemist for a fast-induced headache, say, and find us washing down our *trayf* delicacy with a doubly forbidden milkshake. In fact, I'm afraid, we felt such contempt for the proceedings one block away in the synagogue that our dietary nose-thumbing on these occasions struck us as only mildly naughty.

To the sacrilegious pleasures of forbidden food I soon added those of sex. On Yom Kippur especially, my grandparents' house was certain to be empty of adults. There I took my distant cousin Dolores for the heaviest petting sessions we eight- or nine-year-olds could contrive. And it was in one of the bedrooms of this house that I taught my younger brother to masturbate, having myself been initiated in our own back garden by an older boy, a Roman Catholic who took advantage of the occasion also to tell me some wonderful lies about his Church's funeral practices.

Dolores's exact degree of cousinship eludes me. But her father bore the same name as my own, Hyman Levy. In fact, in this one little town there were three Hyman Levys. 'Hyman' was, of course, simply an attempt to English the Hebrew name Chaim. My father's was the generation in which it was fashionable to give Jewish boys forenames derived from English surnames. So there were not only Hymans, but Irvings, Sheldons, Seymours, Maurices, Herberts and Normans. In such a small place, it became necessary to distinguish between three boys of the same name so close in age. So Dolores's father, who had always been plump, got the unpleasant nickname 'Lardy' Levy. The eldest of the Hyman Levys was the son of a poultry merchant; he, regrettably, was branded for life as 'Chicken' Levy. My lucky father was 'Murph' or 'Murphy', and no one who really knew him ever called him anything else, except for his sisters, who addressed him by his full name, or shortened it, unattractively, to Hymie. The provenance of 'Murphy' was a subject we often discussed. I never heard a satisfactory answer. He was blond and blue-eyed, as we all are; but there's nothing Irish in that. I think I remember his once saying that a schoolmaster had confused him with a boy whose last name really was Murphy, and the incongruous soubriquet stuck.

Chapter Two

My father was born in Lexington in 1911, Joe Levy's son and heir. Anyway, that's what the world thought: my mother's family practically forced her to marry him as they imagined he would come into all the land. They were very wrong; but my parents were divorced well before this question was of any practical importance. Murph – which is what I called him after I outgrew 'Dad' – was bothered by his colouring. It didn't seem properly Jewish to him. Or to the few other Jewish boys at the local elementary and high schools he attended who teased him in a way he minded. He was well educated; in his day the curriculum in southern schools was still identical with what would have been until recently that of a good English grammar school. He learnt the classics, both Greek and Latin and, until his distressingly prolonged final illness, retained a good collection of Latin tags for use when he was in his cups, a condition that often resulted in linguistic inventiveness. Yiddish he learnt at home. The Hebrew liturgy he learnt by rote after school hours from one of the many old rabbis who, even in my own time, had no other idea of how to teach a language, even one as dead as Hebrew was before the foundation of the state of Israel.

Murph must have had a really tough time. American-born, but the child of unassimilated immigrants, who passed none of their own secular culture on to him. He must have longed to be like the other southern boys, whom he more closely resembled physically than he did the other Jewish boys his parents insisted he befriend. He could never have been much good at games – he was only five-foot-three when he was fully grown – although he claimed to play tennis well. On the other hand, he was clever. At high school he did enough science to ease his way into the local university's School of Agriculture. This was the University of Kentucky, whose agriculture department, in those days, was unrivalled by any in the country except Cornell. He was good: many years later, an eminent bacteriologist, whom I met at a party, astonished me by saying that my father had been one of his most promising pupils, and that it was a disappointment to him that he had not made a career in science.

So Joe Levy's son became a *proper* farmer, scientifically trained and a good judge of cattle. You'd expect that Grandfather would realise his own ambitions through his son and hand over the management of the farms straight away. But you'd be wrong. Joe Levy, whether out of meanness or just normal Oedipal malice, did little more than offer to hire my father as a farmhand. Murph never talked about this period, and never spoke ill of his father whom he professed to revere. But I'm certain the old rascal was horrid to him.

Fortunately perhaps, there was not long to wait until the beginning of the war, and alternative employment in a defence plant. There are some lost years, though, and I don't know what my father did between the ages of twenty-two or twenty-three, when he presumably took his BSc in agriculture, and thirty, when America finally entered the war. I wish I had pressed him to tell me; it might have made him kinder to me when I was the same age and as uncertain as he must have been himself.

He never really farmed. He went on to make a bit of money after the war, by having the shoe concession in the town's smartest clothing store, Meyers (which figures often in the subsequent tale), and then a real killing, by virtually inventing the self-service department store. With two other financial backers he opened a large store in a depressing, lower-middle-class suburban location. It had masses of parking, merchandise well bought and cheaply priced, piled high on tables separated by aisles wide enough to allow the passage of a supermarket trolley. Before long he owned the entire block, had bought out his partners, and was accused of having personally been responsible for the commercial death of the city centre. It was, of course, killed not by my father's business activity, but strangled by its inaccessibility to the private motor car.

In his late middle age, he made the great error of handing the business over to my younger brother and tried, in a demoralised fashion, to farm. He pored over stud books of exotic breeds of cattle, debating with himself and the few people who would agree to listen, the merits of Charolais versus Simmental blood to mingle with his herd of pedigree Angus beasts. He once performed a *coup* of back-breeding that resulted in a creature that looked exactly like an Indian cow, with a lovely smooth hide and a hump. This heifer looked so out of place in the Kentucky Bluegrass landscape that it made us laugh to see her. But poor Murph was no better a gentleman farmer than his father Joe had been, and his schemes all came to nought.

Murph had married my mother a year before I was born, on 7 January, 1940, when she was just nineteen and he was twenty-nine. The war in Europe was well under way, and he wasn't keen on becoming a soldier – he always said he had been so bad at military drill in the University of Kentucky Reserve Officers Training Corps that he had been immediately promoted to drill sergeant, so that he could stand apart from the marching cadets, and it wouldn't be noticed that he was incapable of marching in step himself. A married man stood a better chance of avoiding conscription than a single one; it was better still to be a father. So I was born on 26 February 1941, a very much wanted baby. At least by my father. My mother hadn't much choice.

Shirley Betty (she was never Elizabeth) Singer was born in March, 1920, in Cleveland Ohio. She had been a bright student at Henry Clay High School in Lexington, and her teachers had reckoned her to be university material. Shirley thought so too, but her mother and family thought otherwise. She was pretty and had lots of boyfriends (including a dashing gangster from Detroit, photographed in a snappy fedora, double-breasted, padded shoulders suit, and thick-knotted wide tie), especially after she overcame her depression at having moved from big-city Cleveland to this southern hick town where they drawled and used a diffently inflected form of the second person of the personal pronoun. She soon got used to saying 'your all's' for the plural genitive, though, and now speaks with a drawl in which there is no trace of her native Lake Erie midwestern twang. Her mother, Dorothy (whom I christened Tootsie as soon as I could talk, and who was never known by any other name on this side of the family), apparently was worried that Shirley would be an old maid. After all, she, Tootsie, had been married at sixteen. In fact, Shirley says she had plenty of beaux, most or all of them eligibly Jewish. It seems likely to me that her family were more worried about her morals than her marital status, and preferred marrying her off to policing her.

In any case, college was not on the cards. My mother has resented this for her entire adult life. It has to be admitted that she nurses grudges and finds it difficult to forgive or forget a slight that may have happened thirty years earlier. But her lack of education has been a real grief to her. Worse, when, aged forty, she had the leisure and the wealth to resume her interrupted education in the swinging sixties, she found she lacked the motivation to make a go of adult education. Owning race horses, having a clandestine affair (she was still married to her second husband), and spending enough time in the company of Caesar Romero (the Hollywood heart-throb, then in the prime of his unending middle age) to have acquired an entire wall-full of framed photographs of them together — were much more engaging pastimes.

It was my good luck that Shirley was born in Cleveland. It was just as likely to have been Whitechapel, and her son might have found himself born with a Cockney accent instead of a southern drawl. Her own mother, Tootsie, never knew where she was born herself. She had been brought up in Whitechapel, somewhere off the Commercial Road, by a step-mother, and was never told anything about her real mother. She may very well have been born in the East End, but she had no papers, and no memories of anywhere else, with the sole exception of Hyde Park, where she remembered her father taking her. Her flaming red hair (which, thanks to the hairdresser's art, she retained, along with her svelte figure until her death from emphysema in her late seventies) argued Polish blood (red-headed Polish Jews are not uncommon). But perhaps it was the same on her side of the family as on my father's side: we were patently more Slavic than Semitic. Several or maybe all my great-great-grandmothers must have been raped by Cossacks. It was much more common than pedigree-proud Jews would admit; and, because of Jewish matrilineal descent, caused few practical problems. The father may have been ginger-haired or blond, green- or blue-eyed; it mattered not, for nine months later, out popped a little Jew.

Whether born or just sojourning in Whitechapel, my grand-mother would have been condemned to a hard life there. When she visited me in Oxford in 1970, I took her to London two or three times, and we made desultory attempts to explore the area around the Commercial Road, in search of her house and her school. Curiously enough, the small road where her house had been was still shown in the current 'A–Z', though the street was most definitely no longer there. It had been bombed in the war and effaced from the surface of the earth, though not from the map.

She was not sentimental about it and made only the most casual effort to contact the family who had remained behind in Whitechapel (and which, I later learnt, was at least as large in numbers as our big American cousinage). Tootsie had a few pleasant or amusing memories of her East End girlhood, such as the Jewish pawnbroker friend of her father's, who claimed once to have taken in pawn a watch belonging to the Prince of Wales. ('Tum Tum' was famous for his associations with Jews.) This was meant to have occurred during one of his notorious gambling sessions (though I have never read of his having a penchant for the East End, I don't suppose it's impossible). In my grandmother's story an equerry popped the watch one evening, and returned to redeem it the next day; for his trouble the pawnbroker is supposed to have received the Royal Warrant, 'Pawnbroker to HRH the Prince of Wales'. It's a sweet story.

It didn't seem tactful to pursue family matters as far as my own curiosity would have led us. So my Australian girlfriend and I packed up my grandmother and her travelling companion, a younger first cousin of mine who was not very quick thinking, but whose passionate attachment to Tootsie meant that he would look after her carefully. Their fares and expenses had been paid by my father, who had always remained fond of his ex-mother-in-law; it was one of the most generous things I ever knew him do. We took them off to Paris, where, at La Coupole, Tootsie, who though never kosher, had a few common Jewish food prejudices, said that now she was in her seventies (I reckon she was born in 1895), she would very much like to taste oysters. They were much to her taste; she accounted personally for a dozen size oo Belons, and with equal relish dispatched her first roast partridge, which she had chosen to follow the oysters.

Her escape from Whitechapel was engineered by her husband. At sixteen she was an Edwardian beauty. She was tiny, four foot eleven inches, and had delicate colouring; in photographs taken of her just after her marriage, she looks like a just nubile girl pretending to be grown-up for the camera. She is wearing silk chiffon and a very wide-brimmed hat. She was ravishing. I'm sure my grandfather, Israel Singer, who had known her as a child, could scarcely wait for her to grow up. Izzy married Dorothy, and immediately carried her off to America.

There is a rogue gene on my mother's side of the family. It comes from Izzy, who, my mother discovered only recently, was a bit of a con-man. It makes its inheritors prone to get-rich-quick schemes, and is not conducive to the ordinary, plodding pursuit of one's daily bread. Its unhappy possessors have more ambition than talent, and they lack the virtue of patience. It's not their fault: they can blame it on Izzy. I might have thought it was a sex-linked gene, passed in the female line, but only turning up in the males. That was before I recognised my own youthful impatience in my two daughters. Will I ever be able to teach them to cook? At present they're at the hurry-up stage (which I remember only too well) of thinking that breaking eggs constitutes making the omelette.

I never knew Izzy. He died when he was forty, well before my birth. Indeed, until my mother received and passed on to me the revelation of his malfeasance (from a cousin in California who'd known him well), I don't think I even knew his English name.

I am, naturally, named after him, as he was the most recently deceased male in the family. That is to say, I was given his Hebrew names, Yisroel Pesach. (So was my first cousin, the son of my mother's immediate elder sister Kay. They were pregnant at the same time, and only chose one set of names for a boy, and one for a girl, calculating the odds quite wrongly of there being one child of each sex. My cousin Paul was born thirteen days after me.) I sometimes wish my parents had had the courage to give me my grandfather's proper name, and call me Israel. I think I would have made a good job of it. But they, both born in America, and sensitive to the undercurrent of anti-Semitism in the south where they lived, thought bearing such a defiantly Jewish name would be an intolerable handicap for a child. So, under the misapprehension that Jewish custom required that the Hebrew names and the, as it were, Christian names have the same initials, they gave me a first name that it still gives me acute embarrassment even to write. I was never called by it.

So great was, and is, my aversion to it, that I could not bring myself to comply with the inane but rigid bureaucratic American university entrance system. I simply could not type – or print in block letters – my full name. The resulting tangle of initials was so incomprehensible that my application form and my excellent entrance examination results were filed under quite different names, and I was rejected by every single university to which I applied.

Now that I have succeeded in effacing the hateful appellation from every official document except my birth certificate, I can almost tolerate it. Murph and Shirley, in search of a name beginning with 'I', unhappy with Israel, and, fortunately, aesthetically offended by the common Jewish nominal resort to Irving, named me Irvine – with a terminal 'e'. I hated it; so did Shirley. She blamed it on Murph. But cousin Paul bears the ghastly name as well, and Murph could hardly be responsible for that. Years later I realised who the nominating villain must have been: Tootsie, Dorothy, Whitechapel granny. Irvine is the name of a town in Scotland (and in California). I was cursed with this baptismal burden because of a half-remembered geography lesson that took place in a school somewhere off the Commercial Road.

Though I never knew Izzy, I knew his father. There is a photograph of me and my cousin Paul, aged three or four, each holding the hand of a man wearing a skullcap and a very long beard. That was Chaim Singer, my great-grandfather. The picture was taken in Cleveland, where the old man was still employed as a sacred scribe. He wrote out the scrolls of the Torah in what, by all accounts, was particularly fine calligraphy. (There are a few secular examples of his work in Cleveland, and I believe I remember hearing of a nicely comic family squabble over their ownership.) He had been brought to Cleveland – from where I know not, but Russia, Poland and Whitechapel are all possibles – by his surviving son, my great uncle Harry, whom I remember clearly. I was well-endowed with great aunts, too, for Uncle Harry had sisters Pearl, Minnie and Shirley.

Wonderfully enough, their father, Chaim, had remarried. This pleased no one but him. In fact, it so annoyed my great-aunts that they refused to learn my step-great-grandmother's name. She, consequently, was always called 'She', and in every case, including the vocative. In later years, the great-aunts would grow mirthful, remembering how their self-restricting nominal ordinance forced them to say, 'Give it to She,' 'Shut the door, please, She' 'Come here, She' or 'It's She's turn to do the dishes.' Poor She.

What was the nature of grandfather Izzy's misbehaviour? I don't know what it was, but where it was was Detroit. (There was a short-lived posh resort hotel venture in Mount Pleasant, in which much money was lost by Izzy and his brother Harry.) Harry was a prosperous furrier in Cleveland, and I think we can guess that Izzy's naughtiness had something to do with pelts, as the state of Michigan, with its easy access to Canada, was a centre of fur-trading. Whether Izzy was trying to pull a fast one on the Indian trappers, or merely trying to out-silver fox his brother, I don't know.

Unlike my paternal grandparents, who were spared any contact with the New York Jews they so despised, Izzy and Tootsie came to America the normal way, via Ellis Island. They spent some time in the ghetto of Williamstown, and it was there, Tootsie always claimed, that she acquired her slight Yiddish accent. She worked hard, she told me, to rid herself of her native Cockney, and to exchange it for what she assumed, never at the age of sixteen venturing far away from totally Jewish Williamstown, was a proper American accent. In Cleveland, Ohio, her speech was incongruous. In Lexington, Kentucky, it was bizarre.

Chapter Three

Whatever Izzy's mischief, Tootsie had quite a grand life after they moved to Cleveland. There was a big house, and there were servants. Tootsie had little to do but enjoy her state and look after her children. The eldest, Lillian, was born in 1911, then Kay in 1916, then my mother, Shirley, in 1920, and finally, a son, Emanuel in 1925. When Izzy died of a heart attack – he was short and stocky, definitely the physical type to suffer a coronary – in 1930, he left the family fortunes in a mess. It was also the time of the Great Depression, and though Uncle Harry did what he could to help, his own purse must have been affected seriously by the Wall Street crash. Fur coats are a luxury, even in the cold Cleveland winter. Besides, Uncle Harry had his own family to support: Aunt Frieda and my mother's first cousins Edwin, called Eddie, and Shirley, condemned by my mother's seniority to be known forever within the family as 'Baby Shirley'. Harry was now the head of the family, and, as such, accepted the responsibility for everyone's welfare. I have no doubt that, even in the middle of the Depression, Uncle Harry was making it his business to see that no Singer ever wanted for a new pair of shoes or faced the prospect of a mortgage foreclosure.

Still, after Izzy's death, Tootsie had to find some way of earning money. She was an accomplished needlewoman, so she set herself up as a dressmaker. Sales of pianos always go up in times of economic depression: people need entertainment and, though pianos are expensive, it's cheaper in the end to make music at home than to take the family out. Tootsie shrewdly realised that even in a depressed economy, there was one item of clothing at the expensive end of the market that people would still buy – so she made wedding dresses.

She managed, with plenty of help from her brother-in-law, to keep her family until Lil, now a raven-haired beauty, finished school and was ready to marry, in 1931, at the age of twenty. Her looks caught the attention of the most preposterous, yet wonderful character in this story. No novelist could have invented Uncle Louis; as a character of fiction he would lack verisimilitude.

Born in 1894 or 1895, and therefore a touch older than Tootsie, Uncle Louis was a genuine southerner. He was born in Lexington, the son of Joe Rosenberg, whose pawnbroker's shop was such a source of fascination to me. Uncle Louis was one of a huge brood that also lived on Upper Street, where his mother, a pious Jew always called 'Mamma' Rosenberg, had, if I'm not mistaken, installed the town's ritual bath, the *mikvah* that was a necessity for Orthodox Jews. The Rosenbergs were remarkable for their longevity. Joe lived to be a hundred and one, and his father was a hundred and four when he died. Uncle Louis only made ninety, and he seemed to have had Alzheimer's disease for some time before his death in 1986.

Uncle Louis was untouched by Orthodoxy and untroubled by religion, which he regarded with a sort of distant good humour. He must have been clever, though I think he was not very educated. For by the time he married Aunt Lil, he was exceedingly rich. In 1929, when stockbrokers were supposed to have been jumping out of their Wall Street office windows, Uncle Louis – or rather, Colonel Rosenberg, for he actually used the title of the Kentucky colonelcy he had no doubt bought from Governor Ruby Lafoon – retired. Lil was his second wife. Though his first marriage was never spoken of, except by my father, who disliked him in an amused sort of way, Murph hinted to me that Uncle Louis's first wife had been a gentile gold-digger and that the liaison had only lasted a matter of days. Aunt Lil might have been penniless, but she was gorgeous, and Louis seemed to have enough money for both – indeed enough to support Lil's whole immediate family.

Where did the money come from? He had a string of properties that he rented out to blacks. I can remember as a child going around with him when he collected the rents. By today's standards, they were slums; I'm not so sure that they were that poor by the housing criteria of yesterday. But the rents from being a southern, small town slum landlord could not possibly have allowed Uncle Louis to own his string of racehorses and buy Lil her diamonds and furs. Perhaps he had a share of some family money. The pawnshop was only the headquarters of the Rosenberg family business; they were seriously into real estate. In my youth it was widely (though surely falsely) believed that the Rosenberg brothers owned the properties that housed virtually all the brothels in town. Uncle Louis, though, never seemed to have any business interests in common with his brothers; it was always my impression that his wealth was independent of theirs, and greater. My father once claimed to me that his fortune was founded on diamond smuggling, but I think this was sour grapes, compounded of the fact that Uncle Louis had a couple of jewellery shops and that he and Lil went to Cuba, Mexico and later, Europe, for their holidays. Murph had been to all these places himself, but he still could think of no reason for Uncle Louis to frequent them unless he was up to the sort of no good best done in foreign parts.

It must have been almost immediately after their marriage that Lil and Louis moved to a house on an island in Biscayne Bay, just next to Miami. I saw it once, at a distance. It had belonged to Max Fleischer, the creator of the character of

'Popeye', and its chief feature seemed to be the elaborate burglar alarm system that went off at random. Perhaps they had only taken the house for the racing season at Hialeah, for they were soon back in Lexington, where they brought the whole of the Singer family except Kay, who married a Cleveland boy, Jerome Jacobi.

What did Lil see in Louis, besides financial rescue? In a way, quite a lot. Though he was Lilliputian – only just over five feet tall – this hardly mattered to Lil, who, like her mother, was an inch short of that. With his swarthy complexion and jet black, straight hair, Louis was actually quite dashing. He wore his expensively cut clothes and heavy rings well, too. Besides his short stature, his most noticeable peculiarity was that he had a voice like Lytton Strachey's, which moved alarmingly, in the middle of a sentence, or sometimes halfway through a word, from a booming bass to the high-pitched, almost whistling soprano of a boy whose voice has not yet broken. As he y'alled and drawled like any native-born Lexingtonian, the effect of this was electric and disturbing. He had taste and style, beautiful handwriting and a well-developed eye. Nature had intended him to be a collector, and so he was.

Louis and Lil moved house twenty-five times in the more than fifty years they were married. In my mind's eye I can still conjure up eight or ten of their houses. Each of them was thrilling, a trove of visually stimulating riches, an Aladdin's grotto of stirring objects; and some of them were exciting as houses, either because they were architecturally interesting, or because they were mysterious and secret, with rooms in odd places or back staircases leading to hiding places for a child with imagination.

In a gilded cage a tiny bird sat on a perch; it was covered in real feathers, blue, red and yellow. You wound it up with a brass key, then dropped a coin down a brass chute. With a click, the bird burst into song, flapping its wings gently and cocking its head from side to side. It was the mechanical bird of

Yeats's 'Sailing to Byzantium', 'Set upon a golden bough to sing/To lords and ladies of Byzantium/Of what is past, or passing, or to come,' as I recognised with a *frisson* when I first read it. There was, I think, a larger and a smaller example of the mechanical bird in a cage, and also, an all-metal singing bird that popped up from the top of a gold coffer the size of a cigarette box. Uncle Louis (for Lil always said it was he who had collected these marvellous toys) also had a hoard of music boxes. There were many the size of the bird-box, that tinkled out familiar tunes in the treble; but also one enormous machine with satisfactory bass notes, that was either an ancestor of the gramophone or had been inspired by the invention of the record player. To my eyes, used to an enormous console containing a Victrola, it looked like a primitive phonograph. It was operated by cranking it up, and inserting a large – perhaps seven or eight inches in diameter – perforated thin metal disc. The holes in it triggered a series of combs, whose tines of different lengths produced the musical notes. Harmonies – whole chords – were made by combinations of holes, and there was an optional set of bells, that could be turned on if you wished for, say, 'The Bluebells of Scotland' or a setting of the twenty-third Psalm, which was majestic if you left the bells on.

In the cellar or attic of Uncle Louis's houses, there was a haphazard accumulation of old musical instruments, of which I liked best and coveted most the snare drums, part of the equipment of a marching band. Eventually one of these moved to my own basement; so I must have been granted my wish. Cigar boxes contained spare strings for absent guitars, banjos and fiddles. There were jew's harps to twang, ocarinas to whistle, and, after their trip to Europe in 1951, a superb assortment of German mouth organs.

Each of their houses contained at least one large combination safe, sometimes two, their contents a source of mystery. Did they contain the smuggled diamonds? They certainly lodged what to the child's eye was Lil's fabulous jewellery, twisted ropes of gold, thick cables strung with lapis lazuli, antique necklaces of chunky semi-precious stones, bracelets of sapphires and diamonds, and, more prosaically, the stock left over after the sale of the two shops: diamond engagement rings, no doubt; but a larger quantity of watch straps. From the safe came a tiny ring for me, a fairly thick gold setting for a cabochon of turquoise (or perhaps jade) that I treasured. The stone must have been flawed, or I careless, for it developed a crack, and a splinter fell out of its rounded surface. Did Uncle Louis take it back from me to be mended, or did I just lose it? The safe also yielded another finger ring, another gold band, this time enclosing a square black stone, carved in intaglio with the head of a Greek or Roman warrior. That too broke. I was not a success at wearing jewellery.

There was so much to look at in their houses. The inlaid brass and tortoiseshell table that we over-optimistically called the Boulle table. Turkey carpets and Persian rugs and runners, richly coloured and intricately patterned. An upright lacquered display case with rounded glass contained an array of snuff boxes and bibelots, carved ivory objects, tiny Capodimonte shepherds and shepherdesses, and the odd departure from good taste, such as a miniature potty in fine porcelain. But the best things were the biggest: two enormous Meissen urns, eighteenth-century I think, with a three-dimensional seascape modelled in relief on their surface. Neptune with his gold trident surged up from white-capped blue rollers; I imagined he had just caused the storm that was sinking the galleon with its many sails all furled. Mermaids and dolphins leaped about amongst the waves; and a sea monster undulated on the side opposite Neptune. The urns were perfect; neither the rough-house playing of my brother and me, nor the rowdy behaviour of several generations of spaniels, terriers and poodles ever did a damage to those glorious rococo vessels. How I loved them, how I coveted them, and how I suffered when they had to go to

37

Sotheby's recently to provide a bit of cash for Lil's and Louis's old age. I think Lil took their loss better than I did.

The silver was rococo, German or perhaps even late eighteenth century American. On the dining room table, heavy branched candlesticks flanked an ornate oval bowl with a cobalt blue glass liner that stood on four short legs. It weighed too much for me to lift it until I was eight or nine. There were several canteens of cutlery in different, elaborately crafted designs, just as there were several sets of china and cut-glass wine glasses. Some of these had chased silver feet and matched the Venetian glass decanter, with its silver collar round its thin neck. It always contained sweet sherry, and I was sometimes allowed a very small glass of it at bedtime.

It stood on the sideboard, along with a curious green glass bell, whose handle was a brightly coloured cockerel, its clapper a minuscule, finely wrought, cock's foot, with talons wrapped around a sphere of some translucent green gemstone. Lil used this to summon the cook to bring the food to the table, or to clear it. Lil's cooks were as important to my education as the four universities I have attended; they need some paragraphs to themselves.

This account is deficient in two respects anyway. The first is that, until relatively recently, I never addressed or referred to my aunt as Lil. As I had done my grandmother, I rebaptised Lil from my cradle. Maybe this was the result of linguistic precocity: Tootsie always claimed I began to talk at an unnaturally early age (and have never shut up since, my mother would always add). 'Lil' I could could not mouth; 'Lalla' my aunt became. She put up with this with a good grace; indeed, I think she welcomed this change of name. But with one proviso: its written form, despite its pronunciation, was always to be the more glamorous 'Lola'. Lola pronounced Lalla she was henceforth to all except friends her own age and those who called her 'Miz Rosenberg'. And for us, Lola was enough, without the honorific prefix 'aunt', unless one was talking to Aunt Kay, who was a stickler for correct form. My second remissness is that I neglected to mention the greatest of Uncle Louis's collections.

Lil recently gave me a cutting from the local paper, the *Lexington Leader*, for 'Saturday Afternoon, June 14, 1947'. Page two contains a large photograph of me, wearing a candy-striped tee shirt, staring intently at an object being held at the height of my waist in Uncle Louis's left hand. (Uncle Louis is staring, just as intently, into the middle distance.) The object he's showing me is a painted cast-iron mechanical penny bank. There are a dozen more of them on a white cloth on the table in front of Uncle Louis, and another dozen on the bookshelf behind me. This was by no means the whole of the collection; of the 600 catalogued since the first of these contraptions was made in 1869, Uncle Louis owned fully half. When a pair of brazen burglars carried off almost all of them from their flat on a busy Saturday afternoon sometime in the late 1960s, it was the second largest collection in America, and woefully underinsured at, I seem to remember, $20,000.

The newspaper story (elegantly written by John Hutcheson – I hope he got a job on the *New York Times* or at least the *Louisville Courier-Journal*) says the mechanical banks depict characters that 'walk, jump, eat, kick and resemble a race of pocket-sized citizens stepping out of a child's fairy book to march in parade.' They were immensely cunning. William Tell fired a penny with his crossbow, which invariably knocked the apple off his boy's head. When you cocked the crossbow to fire another coin, the apple sprang back into its place. Teddy Roosevelt shot a penny from his shotgun at a grizzly bear whose head poked out of the top of a hollow tree; the missile went into an opening in the trunk of the tree, triggering the mechanism that allowed the bear to duck to safety. The very ingenuity of these meant that they were not the most valuable in the collection; banks with the *least* action were 'the most expensive because children frequently grew tired of them and destroyed them, Mr Rosenberg explained.'

Jack-on-the-ball was one of the rarest banks: it scarcely did anything. You put the penny in the slot in Jack's pointed cap, whirled him on the pivot that bisected him at the waist, and when the ball on which he was balancing was at the top of the arc, he deposited the penny in the base of the bank. Many of the banks were racist. 'The Dark Town Battery' features three black boys playing softball. Another one is 'cast as an aged Negro man sitting in an old-fashioned arm chair eating his afternoon snack. It operates by placing a penny in the man's outstretched hand, pressing a lever which moves the hand to his mouth, depositing the coin there as he rolls his eyes.' The snack was a slice of watermelon: a stereotype in cast iron.

Uncle Louis ended the interview with a modest boast: '"There are only 600 known types of mechanical penny banks and I have 300 of them," he pointed out. "Henry Ford had started a collection before his death, but I believe my collection is larger."

'"But Henry Ford probably didn't have as much money as you do, darling," Mrs Rosenberg observed.

'Her hobby is flying.'

The reporter caught the mood of my aunt and uncle perfectly. Here it was, a couple of years after the end of the war. They were childless, free of domestic responsibilities, and rich. Self-confident, sybaritic, their lives echoed the wisecracking sophistication of similar couples in Hollywood films.

That winter they took me to Miami. My father came too. We stayed at the art deco Cadillac Hotel – at least Lil and Louis did; I think Murph and I may have stayed somewhere less grand. I got painfully sunburnt, but we missed the worst of the dreadful winter of 1947. This was fairly typical of their lifestyle. Spring and summer in Lexington, winter in Miami, Havana or Acapulco. On more than one occasion they took my brother and me to French Lick, Indiana, a spa where they took the waters and we did God alone knows what.

In 1951 they made the first of their trips to Europe. Am I wrong or did they bring back many of their treasures from that journey? The Louis XVI suite, painted white and gilded, upholstered first in turquoise silk and later re-covered in dusty pink: surely they imported the settee and pair of chairs from France. The war must have been good to them, for their fortunes could never have been higher. Perhaps victory brought a hike in property values in Lexington. In any case, like any eighteenth-century aristocrat returning to England from the Grand Tour, they brought back with them the spoils of war-devastated Europe.

Yet it wasn't all the pursuit of pleasure and objets d'art. Though Uncle Louis grew a little pointed beard that made him feel more at home at the Hotel Lutétia, they travelled beyond the confines of the Left Bank. In a way, they were on a mission to Europe. They visited the Festival of Britain, and they did what they could to assure themselves of the welfare of the Whitechapel family. Lil can have known relatively little about them before this trip; and I don't remember her having much to say about them after she'd met them. Indeed, when Tootsie and I, almost twenty years later, made our perfunctory efforts to find the Whitechapel remnant, Lil was not much help with addresses or even names. I suspect I know why. Though Lil couldn't have articulated this, I think she would have found an unbridgeable social gulf between her and her relations. Though she was perfectly suited to the role of playing overseas Lady Bountiful to our East End cousins, there was a practical limit to what she could do for them. And if my own experience years later held true for her then, she would have found that there was less to talk about than one would imagine. She would have learnt the sad lesson that, in England, even family ties don't transcend class.

(Shirley and I once had a richly comic encounter with one of our distant British cousins. We had winkled her out because one of my mother's Cleveland aunts, my great aunt Pearl, I think, had returned to London for her first visit since emigrating. We found her, and she had in tow *her* cousin. We had an appointment to meet at my Hampstead flat. Four o'clock passed, then five. At half past, an hour and a half late, our newly discovered relative rang my bell. There were no apologies. She had arrived early for our rendezvous, and finding no one there, gone off to visit someone else in Golders Green. Not only did she not share our bourgeois notions of timekeeping, but I noticed that she didn't believe in banks. She had all her wealth on display, her fingers covered in rings, her arms wreathed in bracelets. Once she rang my home number and the telephone was answered by my wife. She was tonguetied with confusion, my East End cousin told me, because she didn't know the proper form of address for my wife: she thought from Penny's voice that she might be 'titled'.)

In France Lil made some life-long friends. I'd be surprised if some of them weren't more than friends. In the late sixties I had arranged to meet Lil and Shirley at La Coupole. My friend and I arrived first. When the ladies came through the door, a stage-Frenchman's cry of 'Li-lee' went up. They had just come on the spur of the moment from England. Lil had not had time to warn her friends of her coming. People at a long table embraced her and shifted their places to make room for us. At the end of the meal I observed that the man sitting next to me was absent-mindedly drawing with a pencil on the paper tablecloth. He had drawn Lil, totally nude. It was a good likeness.

Lil and Louis really zipped around Europe in 1951, though they were away for months. I remember with pleasure a handkerchief that said 'Nice'; I looked it up in the atlas and, having no clue to its pronunciation, thought it a curious name for a city. From this trip, or one of the many subsequent ones, I received an intricately knitted, patterned ski sweater from

Denmark that I cherished. Packets of stamps and fistfuls of foreign coins came my way too.

But it was 1951, only six years after the end of the war, and as Lil and Louis were, after all, Jewish (though it was certainly not the most important thing about them), they did their duty and took themselves off to Germany. Dachau and Belsen made their impression; and the photographs they took with their newly bought Leica jolted me into as real an understanding of what it was all about as was possible for a ten-year-old. Back in Paris, a cable from Lexington finally caught up with Lil. It asked her to accept the presidency of the Lexington chapter of the National Council of Jewish Women, and meant a real commitment of time and energy. After what she'd seen, she could not refuse.

For all this, there was something foolish and childlike about Uncle Louis, and to the mind of a real child, even something sinister. To an impressionable child he seemed an old man, of the sort who shows an inordinate interest in children's genitals; with amusement, he would call attention to the fact that a baby's penis was very small, to the usually tolerant embarrassment of its parent or his interlocutor. I recall just such a scene; it made me cringe with remembered resentment for the many times he had given my infant willie a tweak or bottom an apparently affectionate pinch. As a child I was also worried by his habit of burning incense and joss sticks in the loo. On the other hand, his bathroom was a place of interest, just as much as any other room in the house. I never lost my fascination for the device for sharpening safety razor blades, which went flip-flop up and down a taut string; or for the self-sharpening one (was it called a Rolls razor?) in its self-contained metal case. It was this man, with his foibles and his bibelots who was supposed to have been the financial saviour of my mother's family by bringing them to Lexington.

I doubt it. I think it was Lil who told her love-struck

husband that he was about to acquire a surrogate family consisting of her mother and two teenaged children. Lil had intelligence and a strong will; Uncle Louis never stood a chance. It was Lil who ran the businesses, Lil who wrote the cheques, Lil who made all the decisions that mattered, but who indulged Uncle Louis in the things that really mattered to him – his collections and an unfailing supply of cream for his breakfast cornflakes. And it was Lil who recompensed him with years of real devotion when he was over eighty and capable of maddening anyone who would listen by asking the same question six or seven times in a row or getting silly from one small drink. She had to police him, but she saw to it that he was comfortable and dignified. Uncle Louis never complained about taking in Lil's family; he used to drawl his laments for the absent 'Miz Singer' long after Tootsie had decided she couldn't take any more of living with him, and was re-housed, aged sixty or so, in a not very agreeable flat in Miami Beach. She, of course, abided by the same code, and never uttered a syllable of dispraise of him.

Uncle Manuel, too, showed proper gratitude and fell in with the fiction of giving the credit for the family's rescue to Uncle Louis. Or rather, to 'the Colonel', for Manuel seldom called him anything else. In this he followed the practice of Uncle Louis's black tenantry. But I'm reminded by the yellowing bit of newspaper with the tale of Uncle Louis's mechanical banks that it wasn't all that unusual for southern gents with the Governor's commission (as aides-de-camp) to style themselves Colonel; the obverse of the cutting contains the front page news of the admission to hospital of 'Col. Matt J. Winn, 85-year-old turfman and Kentucky Derby impresario.' And we mustn't forget Colonel Sanders, whose handle had the same origin as Uncle Louis's.

Manuel went to Henry Clay high school, where he was an accomplished clarinet player, and I think played in a dance band. It must have been a scene right out of a forties high school film. Sixteen at the time of Pearl Harbour, he began his college career before his military service as an Air Force navigator, during which he saw some action abroad. His return to college was another movie: dances, fraternities, dates. I lived through it all vicariously and enjoyably. He lived with the Colonel and his sister until the war.

So did my mother. It wasn't her idea of a good time. After moving to Lexington, much against her will I expect, Shirley naturally came to look upon her time in Cleveland as a Golden Age. It may be difficult to look upon Cleveland as the epitome of Bright Lights and Big City, but I can tell you that for those of us used to the cultural (and culinary) shortages of Lexington, it was Gotham on Lake Erie. For someone making the voyage in the opposite direction, Lexington would have looked like one of the circles of Hell Dante didn't know about, the American equivalent of being transported to Van Diemen's Land. To the twelve- or thirteen-year-old Shirley, Lexington was just a place with a bad summer climate and very few amenities, populated by people, both black and white, who spoke a barely intelligible dialect. Her urbane contempt for them and their country ways was matched only by her bewilderment at having to live amongst them. The result was that the bright and lively Cleveland schoolgirl became a shy and timid (and I shouldn't be surprised to learn, sullen) high school student at Henry Clay. Academically, she was a year ahead of her southern classmates. Socially, she was backward, a Ruth among the alien corn liquor.

It took a couple of sympathetic teachers to help her peck her way out of her shell. Eventually she taught herself to speak as though she had a mouthful of honey, to make every vowel a diphthong, the first milestone on the road to becoming a southern belle. But, of course, Shirley could never have gone all the way down the track: something hard and northern inside her whispered that all that was foolish. In a crisis she could be as tough as Scarlet O'Hara, and as calculating: she could learn to drawl, but not to simper. She began to make friends, mostly among the few other Jewish girls, and when Tootsie and Lil would allow it, to go out with the brothers of her new girlfriends. There, of course, was the rub. She had two mothers.

In retrospect, Shirley, who did well at Henry Clay, wishes she had gone to university. Did she really want to at the time? There were boys to date and money to be made – both steps in the direction of independence. Her first jobs were naturally at Uncle Louis's jewellery shops. She would have graduated from school at seventeen or eighteen; at nineteen she was married to Murph, pushed into it, she always felt with resentment, by her mother and sister. It is easy enough to see their points of view.

Shirley has an anarchic streak in her. Not exactly rebellious, she does what is demanded of her and then fans a spark of indignation in her heart, which smoulders though it seldom bursts into flames. Left to her own devices, Tootsie and Lil probably thought, she would make an unsuitable marriage – or worse, no marriage at all. There was something about the quality of Shirley's admiration for Ingrid Bergman's bravery during her marital plight that convinced me that Shirley at least hoped that she would have been capable of doing the same thing, unthinkable as it was in America in 1940 to live with a man out of wedlock. Tootsie was married at sixteen; she considered that her daughters would become old maids if they left it too much longer than that to marry themselves. Lil may have felt that she had made a sacrifice for the family by her marriage. Why shouldn't Shirley accept the apparent security offered by marriage to Murph? Anyway, Murph was a good catch – the best in town. Shirley collects grudges: her longest-standing one is that her family 'forced' her to marry my father.

Chapter Four

Lexington got its name from the town in Massachusetts that was the scene of the Revolutionary War battle. It was first settled in 1775 or early the next year, though the area had been explored well before that. Kentucky – the word means 'dark and bloody ground' in one of the Indian languages, did not become a state until 1792, when it was number fifteen, after the thirteen original colonies plus Vermont. Daniel Boone (1734–1820) was the most important figure in the early history of both state and town, and was responsible for a number of early fortifications, several of which still exist. The area is rich in historical buildings, all well looked after, and we visited all of them when I was a child.

Daniel Boone was a particularly vivid character to me in childhood, because Boonesborough was the name of the tiny outpost on the Kentucky River, fifteen or twenty miles from Lexington, where for a couple of golden summers we shared with friends of Murph a 'camp', a ramshackle wooden summer house, perched precariously high above the river, with a magical boathouse that accommodated a dinghy with an outboard motor. This was only a few miles beyond our own farms at Athens, but it took me a long time to make the geographical connection. From the colonial period (1774) there was also Fort Harrod at Harrodsburg, an almost completely preserved large garrison used by the early settlers – mostly spill-overs from Virginia, ranging from younger sons of peers to transported convicted felons – when they were setting about their programme of systematically stealing the land from the Indians – mostly the Iroquois, I fancy. They came in defiance of a royal proclamation of 1763 that had prohibited settlement west of the Appalachians. Kentucky had been part of the inaccessible territory beyond the mountains, and at first the French showed as great an interest in it as the British.

Also dating from the Colonial period, I'm pretty sure, was Shakertown. The Shakers' schism with the Quakers was in 1747. This cult, with its furniture and houses of exquisitely simple design that so appeal to modern eyes, and their lovely music (the 'Shaker Hymn' gave Aaron Copland the theme for his 'Appalachian Spring' and is the tune of 'Tis a gift to be simple, 'tis a gift to be wise' and of 'Lord of the Dance') belies their religious mania. They not only shook with holy ecstasy, from which they took their name, but practised the primitive Christian socialism of common ownership of property. This admirable doctrine was conjoined, however, with their embracing the rest of the Albigensian heresy: they practised total celibacy, and replenished their numbers solely by the adoption of children, who were then condemned to this fruitless if aesthetically satisfying existence. As they expected to do, they died out; but the last of our local Shakers lived into the twentieth century.

The Federal period left even more monuments scattered around Lexington and surrounding Fayette County. (The Marquis de Lafayette was our most important Revolutionary war hero; but after his return to France to be the head of the National Guard in his own revolution, he must have relished the irony of the colonists' tribute to him of naming the next county along 'Bourbon county' – of which the seat was, of course, Paris. Lexington also has a small satellite town called Versailles, pronounced Vur-sales.) Most important to my childhood was Ashland, the home of our local hero, Henry Clay (1777–1852), who should have been President several times but for his impolitic inability to compromise (or so we were taught at school). He managed to hold the office of Secretary of State from 1825–29. And he built a magnificent small Georgian country gentleman's house on the Richmond Road north of Lexington.

By the time of my birth the town had so expanded that Ashland was relatively close to the downtown city centre, and there was another group of rich men's grand houses stretching for half a mile further up the Richmond Road. Ashland was set in a park occupying what was to become an entire city block; on every side there were mature pin oak trees, and the gentle slopes of the ground meant you could not quite see from one end of the property to the other. It completely satisfied the ideal of *rus in urbe*, and I loved it. The best thing about it was its ice house. I don't think I saw snow before the terrible winter of '47, when we slid on the pavements until the spring thawed the ice (and I didn't see real snow and ice – or a pair of ice skates – until I visited a friend in Des Moines, Iowa, the winter when I was twelve). I simply could not imagine where the ice to fill the underground bunker could have come from. I knew that some people still had ice boxes and got daily deliveries of ice – I had even seen the refrigerated ice plant where it was made. But my southern mind-set didn't allow me to think that Nature could have provided for Henry Clay's ice house.

Smack in the middle of downtown Lexington was an entire Georgian square, Gratz Park. The Gratzes were the first Jews in Lexington – German Jews, of course, as the Jews of Germany emigrated to America much earlier than those from further east. Benjamin Gratz, though, came from Philadelphia, and was one of Lexington's first gentleman settlers. The family was well-connected – it was always said that his daughter Rebecca was Scott's model for the heroine of *Ivanhoe*.

The Gratzes intermarried with the local gentry, especially, I always understood, with the Clays. Once I remember seeing two thin and dignified old ladies at the Yom Kippur service at the Reform Temple and being told their name was Clay. They were sisters, spinsters, Jewish by virtue of their Gratz blood, which they acknowledged by coming to Temple once a year. The family of Cassius Clay, later Muhammad Ali, were also descendants of the Clay family (whose family names were Henry, Cassius and Lucius), as Henry Clay had kept slaves. Much though we regretted Henry Clay's moral lapse in being a slave owner, it sardonically amused my rebellious friends and me to think that many of the great man's issue were either Jewish or black.

Benjamin Gratz's own house was, I think, no longer still standing. But at the south-western corner of the square (which is, in fact, a rectangle) is the glorious John Hunt Morgan house. Morgan was a Confederate cavalryman, who conducted guerrilla raids across the southern borders after 1862, when the state had been all but pacified. The house dates from the earlier Federal period, with its beautiful Georgian fan-light over a front door, which can be opened to half its width again – some say so as to admit a man while seated on a horse. This might, though, be a myth that has grown up, because Morgan was the local favourite subject of the equestrian statuary that is an essential part of the visual furniture of every southern town. The chief glory of the Hunt Morgan house is the original furniture, made to the designs of Georgian pattern books, but in wonderful native fruitwoods, especially cherry.

A pavilion stands in the square itself and, if memory serves me, it could be hired for children's parties. We no longer went to parties there after I reached the age of nine or ten. I don't know whether this was because the downtown had become unfashionable, or because our parents had come to think air-conditioning a necessity for the seasons of the year during which Gratz Park was a suitable venue for parties. There are some other good Federal houses on the square, and one or two gracious antebellum houses in the Greek Revival style, especially Morrison Hall of Transylvania College (properly called Transylvania University, though we never did), which stands at the north end of the square.

Transylvania (whose Bram Stoker overtones were not lost on me – though to giggle about Dracula was to invite charges of academic snobbery from those who were pleased to be students there) was the first institute of higher learning west of the Alleghenies, and the town was proud of this little four-year liberal arts college, though its facilities were eclipsed by (and it was academically inferior to) the mighty land-grant state University of Kentucky only a few blocks to the south. Also north of Gratz Park was the public library, a Carnegie foundation I think, in whose open stacks I whiled away many an afternoon or Saturday morning. (I've always been attracted by the semi-disciplined allure of somebody else's arrangement of books, and find myself all too easily distracted by them from whatever purpose has brought me amongst them. During my own academic career I made several fruitful discoveries simply by loitering without heuristic intent, but because I was diverted by books on the open shelves of a library.)

Mary Todd Lincoln's birthplace was a little Georgian house not much bigger than a cottage on West Main Street. The President was born in Kentucky as well as the shrew he married – a log cabin stands in the grounds of Transylvania: but surely that is not the famous log cabin of Abraham Lincoln himself? This, then, was the architecture of my early childhood. Antebellum houses – or those modelled on them – were not uncommon; and the domestic vernacular adaptation of Greek Revival resulted in some hilarious, but sinfully ugly suburban boxes, their columns straining to relieve them from squatness, but only making them the more ludicrous. Though civic, not domestic, such a building was the courthouse, faced in some hideous non-local yellow stone. It had its equestrian statues, the blue-green copper colour of every such cast metal object in every southern town; and, as happened everywhere else, at least once a year some wag would paint the horse's balls bright red.

The precincts of the courthouse were always full of good ol'
boys, drinking bottled Coca-Cola from the vending machine
(which once made a mistake and, for my nickel, gave me ten ice
cold bottles of Coke and 85 cents in change). I suppose they
were unemployed – they were, of course, white – and just
passing the time of day with the police, whose business
brought them to the building regularly. The police were racist,
uneducated and unattractive; just like the good ol' boys except
that they were armed. The good ol' boys kept their shotguns
and rifles at home. I don't ever remember hearing of a lynching
in Lexington, but the Klan was certainly active, if secret. We all
believed (wrongly, I am sure) that someone important in the
administration of my high school was a member of the Klan,
and I had heard the curious tale that the Jewish father of one of
my friends had joined the Klan in the twenties to expedite his
political ambitions. How could they have had him? Their
family name wasn't particularly Jewish. Perhaps the masked
men did not know that one of the circumcised was concealed
beneath the white sheet.

What brought me downtown at least one afternoon a week
was the torture session with the orthodontist (I think that is
still the euphemism). The dentist who tightened the wires that
bound my teeth to each other, and so shifted their alignment,
was a thoroughly disreputable old soak with an office very
near the courthouse. Dr Pullet stood over his young patients,
cementing painful thin metal bands on to newly sprouted
permanent teeth, breathing sour fumes on us, that I now
realise were a mixture of fags and booze. It should really have
been obvious even to a ten-year-old that he was nipping at
more than the bottle of mouthwash, for he was as thin as could
be, and had a particularly unsteady hand for a dentist. It hurt –
really hurt. And it wasn't much good for the teeth, either.
When he removed the bands, well after I was in high school,
Dr Pullet managed to take large chunks of my top front teeth
out with them, undoing the cosmetic effects of his own work in

a single gesture per tooth. Moreover, he refused to believe that my last molars, the 'wisdom' teeth, could be making an appearance when I was still adolescent. So at sixteen I had to go to hospital to have four impacted wisdom teeth removed. They had crowded my lower jaw so much that I became snaggle-toothed in a matter of weeks, though my father had spent several thousand dollars, and Dr Pullet quite a few of his relatively sober hours, straightening exactly the teeth affected. This was an essential part of an American childhood in the fifties, but I would have given it a miss if I could have done.

The good ol' boys could also be found (and so sometimes could I) seated at the lunch counter or in one of the booths of Walgreen's drugstore, where fried grits was still on the breakfast menu until I grew up. Or you might find them – or me – at the soda fountain of McAdams and Morford, also on Main Street. I expect we were drinking a Coke with a slurp of cherry or vanilla syrup in it with lots of crushed ice. If it was lunchtime, we might be making ourselves sick with a chilli dog, a particularly poor quality pork-and-cereal hot dog in a pappy white bun, with a drizzle of spicy chilli con carne on it. If you squirted on plenty of French's mustard from the yellow plastic globe with a nozzle, and added lots of chopped raw onion, it was delicious.

Who were these louts that sat around doing nothing all day? I don't remember. Some of them could have still been at school – if they were at a different school than mine, there would be no reason for me to know their faces. (These, it seems unnecessary to add, were universally white. Public places were segregated in practice, if not in law.) Probably they were just the lumpenproletariat – whose ranks must have been swollen considerably by returning war veterans who had neither skills nor jobs. These same faces could be seen in summer at Joyland, the amusement park at the northern extremity of the town. They seemed menacing, as groups of older men and boys always do to the younger; but I don't really remember any untoward incidents.

Joyland was wonderful. It had a dance floor, and I think our parents may sometimes have gone there after dark, to dance the jitterbug and drink beer. But that was of no interest to us children. The prime attraction was the swimming pool; and I can still shut my eyes and see myself being given lessons by Ada Gail, the mother of my friend Mitchell. She taught me to float on my back and on my tummy, and not to be afraid. Shirley, though not so authoritatively confidence-making, taught me to swim too. And she rubbed into my pale skin a home-made mixture of Johnson's baby oil and iodine that was supposed to induce a tan – and probably did dye the skin with the indelible iodine dispersed in the globules of oil. Joyland, however, was a full-fledged amusement park, not just a swimming bath. There were rides: the cissy carousel and the big dipper roller coaster with its seeming miles of track mounted on white stilts. It was understood that we were so terrified of it that no one ever so much as suggested a ride on it.

What need had we of it? There were dodgem cars; for a nickel or a dime you could take part in licensed mayhem, in which the rules of the road only existed to be broken. There was a boat ride – was it called the ghost ride? – in which scary noises made you huddle closer to the person next to you on the seat, and phosphorescent spooks would suddenly appear in the dark that was randomly illumined by lightning-like flashes, and nameless wet things would, without warning, smack you in the face. It was bliss, and remained so until I was ten or eleven. Then, miserable fat boy that I was, I got a masochistic kick from the Hall of Fun, with its distorting mirrors, and the air-jets that lifted the girls' skirts and went whoosh up your trouser legs. And the games. The best was called skeet ball. It was a cross between a pin-ball machine and a bowling alley and involved gently and accurately throwing a heavy wooden ball up an inclined plane. At the top of the slope were a series of holes surrounded by a semi-circle of bent plywood, each bearing a number, which was the value of getting the ball in that particular opening. I think you got the ball back for another go if you got it in one of the numbered holes; otherwise it fell away into a gutter at the top and sides of the slope. There were the normal fairground prizes for high scores; and though I was not adept at games, I quite often won one of these intrinsically not very valuable objects.

Except for going to the movies, there wasn't really much to do for the good ol' boys. They probably couldn't afford the brothels with which the town was supposed to teem. I never actually even learnt the location of any of these, and wonder whether their rumoured existence was not really an imaginary homage to history. For Lexington had once had the most famous fancy house between New York and New Orleans.

Belle Breezing's whorehouse was not a myth. In my young day there were men who spoke of it as though they had knowledge by acquaintance and, in any case, the establishment has been well documented by local historians, including William H. Townsend, a Lincoln scholar, whose privately printed pamphlet of 1966, 'The Most Orderly of Disorderly Houses', I have in front of me. The three storey brick mansion was on the south-west corner of Wilson and Megowan Streets (the latter has been renamed Northeastern Avenue). It flourished between 1890 and 1917, when the US Army closed it, after having established Camp Stanley quite close to the town.

Belle Breezing served her own professional apprenticeship in a cat house located in the West Main Street, Mary Todd Lincoln House; she lived on in the crumbling ruins of her own Gay Nineties house until her death on 11 August, 1940. She is buried in a cemetery on West Main Street, 'where rest a number of her former "girls" and several gentlemen procurers', in graves marked by 'a lone granite shaft, eight feet tall', bearing the inscription, 'Blessed be the Pure in Heart'. There is quite a lot of information about Belle Breezing because, when she died, *Time* magazine gave her nearly the entire obituary column.

Her house was purpose-built for what the local newspaper called 'the most mundane of sublunary pastimes'. According to Bill Townsend, 'It was located in the heart of the "red light" district, which occupied the high ground north of Main Street and extended from the bridge over the C & O [Chesapeake and Ohio Railway] tracks along Megowan to Second Street.' One hell of a distance. But one can see why. It was crowded: 'In addition to Miss Belle's place, the houses of such well known Madames as Blanche Patterson, Lizzie Hill, "Mother" Board, Barb Burnell, "Snooky" Simson, and other less pretentious establishments lined both sides of the street just about all the way.' No wonder that, when I was an adolescent, we were so convinced that there were brothels abounding, only awaiting discovery. It was in the town's traditions – it was in the very air.

Belle Breezing's was Lexington's first tourist attraction; 'sporting men' from all over the country used to come expressly to dally with Belle's girls. Belle was the model for 'Belle Watling', the Madame in *Gone with the Wind*. She was also the Madame Claude of her day; she made sure her ladies could make conversation as well as they made love, and the girls were dressed as stylishly as the premises were decorated.

Her wine cellars were well stocked with vintage Champagne and other French wines, as well as 'whiskeys – never reduced in proof by being "bottled in bond", but drawn directly from the spigots of aged, oaken barrels racked in the cool, spacious wine cellar in the basement'. Called to Miss Breezing's house by her doctor, when she was near death and wished to give her books to the University library, Bill Townsend discovered a 'Circassian walnut secretary' that housed two large morocco-bound photograph albums.

'The very first one was truly amazing – inscribed "My

56

Opening Night, 1891" – a long, sumptuously appointed banquet table, extending the entire length of the three parlours all thrown together, exquisite linens, gleaming silverware, dazzling cut glass, fragile china, tall vases of American Beauty roses, an orchestra behind potted palms in a far corner. At the table sat beautiful young women, appropriately costumed for such an auspicious occasion, and, incredible as it seems today, doctors, lawyers, businessmen, civic and social leaders of the city – quite a number of whom I had known, and known well, when I first came to the bar – all immaculately clad in full dress suits, making no effort whatever to conceal their identity.'

Until my adolescence, downtown Lexington had its elegant aspect as well as its courthouse sleaze. On Main Street there were smart department stores, Purcell's, Wolf Wiles's and Stewart's; Lowenthal's furriers; Hymson's Tots and Teens was cornily named, but sold expensive kids' gear. Above all there was Meyers, riding outfitters, and arbiters of taste for both men's and women's clothes. For a time after the war, Murph had the large shoe concession there. (I suppose he was making a show of independence to his father; it wouldn't have needed much capital to start up. He was leasing the space from a great friend; and his brother-in-law Max Kraus, Jenny's husband, was a shoe wholesaler in Cincinnati, so Murph's credit would have been good. He was almost bound to make a success of it, and he did.) Most of these businesses were owned by Jews.

'Downtown' still meant something, even through the Eisenhower years. My mother would not have dreamt of going downtown unless she was dressed properly, which meant wearing or carrying a pair of short white gloves and, of course, wearing a dress. The rites of habiliment were taken seriously, a thing transplanted Yankees, accustomed to wearing any old thing at all on the streets of Manhattan or Detroit, could never

57

understand. I am sure the first middle-class woman to wear a pair of shorts on Main Street was not born or brought up in Lexington.

(A few years ago, I gate-crashed a party at which the Prince and Princess of Wales were present. I had just come to my office from the country, and was wearing my country clothes. One of my editors had a spare invitation for the 'do' at the Royal Academy, and invited me along. When the speeches were about to be made, security men brusquely rounded up the crowd, with the result that I was placed directly in front of the Princess's seat on the platform – the only object in her line of vision. I suddenly became conscious that I was wearing brown shoes – in town, and in front of royalty. I felt the blush spreading, hot across my face: in imagination I was a small boy again, improperly dressed to go downtown. My mother, I thought, would have killed me.)

With Shirley in her white gloves and me in long trousers, we might treat ourselves to a genteel luncheon in the dining room of either the Phoenix or the Lafayette Hotel, where we were known by name to every single one of the black waiters in their white jackets. Or there was the more sophisticated, even slightly louche Golden Horseshoe restaurant, also on Main Street. This was owned – or at least run by Ralph Campbell (who later ran the elegant and smart Campbell House Hotel and restaurant on the town's southern outskirts). Unlike the hotel dining rooms, the Golden Horseshoe was the sort of place a man could take his mistress – or court his girl, if he was sufficiently well-heeled. The banquettes were upholstered in real red leather, as was the horseshoe-shaped bar, and the white waitresses Ralph employed also knew our names – even my brother's and mine.

In memory, the food was wonderful. In fact, it probably wasn't bad. There was the ubiquitous southern-fried chicken, using the original, simple recipe of shaking pieces of good quality chicken in seasoned flour in a paper bag, and deep-frying it in very hot vegetable fat or lard until it was golden and crisp on the outside, and still moist inside. I still cannot understand why Col. Sanders's minions have perverted this recipe with herbs, spices and (no doubt) MSG; it's just not as good as the cheaper, pure version. There was always country ham, too; brine-cured, at least a year old and attacked by mysterious moulds as it aged in its paper bag cover in the cellar. Kentucky ham has a salty tang and the not entirely disagreeable texture of overcooked roast beef. But it was more common to order fried chicken and country ham (with teeth-cracking 'beaten biscuits') at the country inn restaurants at Berea and Harrodsburg. They were unlicensed and you drank iced tea served in great jugs – or went home thirsty.

There was steak and roast beef, too, always on the menu in these licensed restaurants downtown; but, as is still the case, the patrons were more likely to drink a cocktail or a whiskey or two before the meal, than to drink anything during it. Beer was sometimes ordered with food, but I don't think wine was even available until the late sixties. Every eating place in town was capable, mysteriously, of serving a thick, hot but rare slice of 'Prime Rib'. The best bit came with the rib attached, with its crisped fat and chewy, caramelised shreds of meat next to the bone. It was always served 'au jus', which meant that somebody had tampered with the pan juices to turn them into a thin gravy.

Sometimes, especially in the hotel dining rooms, there were seasonal delicacies, such as the floured and lightly sautéed shad's roe, served on toast with a wedge of lemon. But we were landlocked; fish was rare, and shellfish non-existent, except for soft-shell crabs, which we seemed to get in their season every year. I think this was before the advent of freezers in restaurants, so someone must have imported the crabs from Maryland, packed in ice. Their journey south and west from Chesapeake Bay, by truck, was a long one. I suppose Lexington was just one stop on the soft-shell crab delivery itinerary.

When I was four, Lil drove *me* in the car the ninety miles to Louisville to eat my first lobster. (Louisville was big enough for its airport to receive flown-in live Maine lobsters.) My infantile enactment of the eating scene from *Tom Jones* took place at Brown's Hotel, and I'm sure my education was not Lil's only reason for undertaking such a serious journey. It was the end of the war and she must have been starved for delicacies. Brown's Hotel gave its name to another regional dish that figured on the menu of all Lexington's top eateries: the Hot Brown was (and is) an elaborate, open hot sandwich that starts with toast, on which are layered slices of turkey breast, covered in a cheese sauce (Ralph Campbell would have called it *mornay*), topped with rashers of crisply grilled bacon. If there are a few grains of cayenne in the sauce, and the turkey is only yesterday's leftovers and not last week's, the dish is a worthy one.

Lamb from the Bluegrass region is a great gastronomic treat; it derives its special flavour, we understood, from the grass itself, *Poa pratensis*, which only truly flourishes in the area around Lexington. This, in turn, has something to do with the limestone content of the soil. In any case, the lamb is good and, being both good and in short supply, goes mostly to the tables of New York City's restaurants. Ralph Campbell used to get a little bit of it, and the double, thick broiled loin chops at the Golden Horseshoe were memorable. The limestone was also responsible for the costly Kentucky Bibb lettuce, a softer cos-type that, dressed only with a vinaigrette and never the Roquefort sauce made with unsweetened mayonnaise that is reserved for iceberg lettuce wedges or mixed salads, made a noble salad course – served at the beginning of the meal, of course.

The potato baked in its jacket and served with soured cream and chives was a treat, and not the universal starchy offering it has become. With grilled meat there were wonderful French fried potatoes, thick and crisp, or shoestring potatoes, miraculously thin and long. Mashed potato, made properly with hot milk and butter, was common, as were gratins made with cream but no cheese. Green beans were always overcooked, but sometimes with cubes of kosher garlic salami, to a recipe that has become southern rather than Jewish; and sometimes, but rarely, there were greens done the soul food way with bits of ham hock. Corn was more likely to make an appearance as a savoury pudding, bound in an eggy soufflé mixture, than on the cob.

The breadrolls were always baked on the premises. Everybody's favourite was the Parker House roll, that looked like a muffin, but split into several thin vertical buttery leaves. Never, ever would you see on Ralph Campbell's menus a first course or side order of tinned fruit salad or one of those southern gothic edible horrors, the 'moulded' salad whose chief ingredient was the sweet, synthetically flavoured Jello. Sometimes his food was not sophisticated, but it was always real food.

Desserts were southern: pecan pie, made with sweet Karo corn syrup, chess (pronounced chezz) pie, which always seemed to me just a version of the same pie without nuts; Nesselrode parfait or pie, a mixture of real-cream vanilla ice cream with rum-preserved fruits. Heady and delicious but puzzling: how did this mixture come to be named after a nineteenth-century Russian diplomat?

We had other, lesser restaurants. The Canary Cottage, on the corner of East Main Street in Ashland Avenue, served dainty things for ladies' luncheons and children's portions. Leavis's restaurant started life as a Greek greasy spoon, but progressed to becoming a smart, masculine downtown eatery, where only the generous Greek salad with black olives and feta cheese and the mild pickled green chillies remained to give a clue to its ethnic origins. The Little Inn was spoken of in terms that made me think it might have been a speakeasy during Prohibition. In my day we called it a roadhouse – it was a good distance away from the downtown on the Winchester Road – and it served local delicacies such as country ham and lamb fries i.e., testicles. For lamb fries, plus fried catfish and those leaden balls of fried dough called hushpuppies we went to Hall's on the river at Boonesborough. At Chef Sear's, miles out on the Nicholasville Road, we ate chopped sirloin steak served in such large portions that I always found it indigestible.

To revert for a moment to the subject of drink. When I was a child, most grown-ups drank Bourbon. This was made locally – though not entirely in Bourbon County – and never, *never*, in Tennessee. Jack Daniels, we heard repeatedly, was *not* Bourbon; it was Tennessee whiskey. Bourbon had by law to be made in Kentucky. It was drunk with 'branch water' which, in my pre-chlorinated and -fluoridated childhood days, was water from any old tap in Lexington. It was delicious water, pure, with a perfectly clean flavour. Bourbon and branch was drunk from a heavy, real silver tumbler with a rim called a julep cup. Julep cups were expensive. They were given for birthday presents to older children, as trophies in sporting events and, especially, as wedding presents. We all had our collections of julep cups. I still do.

You can recognise a Lexington *Landsman* instantly by seeing the contents of his flat. I did just that recently in a smart, spacious flat on London's Chelsea Embankment, when I was able to tell our host of our shared origins merely on the strength of his tell-tale set of julep cups. When my mother married for the second time, her new husband brought with him an annual case of Heaven Hill Bourbon, a Christmas present from his generous cousins called Shapiro, who, I think, made the stuff. It had the effect of devaluing the currency: my family switched to drinking Scotch, as was fashionable.

Still, twice a year, we all, even the children, drank Bourbon. The first occasion was the Kentucky Derby, always the first Saturday in May. Mint juleps were made by 'muddling' fresh mint leaves with sugar in a julep cup, topping it up with an unthinkably large slug of Bourbon – a julep cup holds eight or ten fluid ounces – leaving it to 'marry', and then serving it frosty from being filled to the brim with crushed ice, so that it is too cold to hold in an ungloved hand. The children were given a sip: any more of this sweet, child-appealing stuff would certainly have resulted in tight tots.

We did get tight, and usually sick, too, at Christmas and the New Year, when most Lexington families followed the same custom as Lil, and got out the heavy silver punch bowl. It was filled – for the visitors who called continuously for the week from Christmas Eve until New Year's Day – with egg nog. The recipe called for six whole eggs, I think, to a quart of milk, a pint of heavy cream, sugar, nutmeg and half a 'Fifth' bottle of Bourbon. Its lethal properties were not diminished by the food that normally accompanied it: slivers of salty country ham between buttered halves of hardtack-like beaten biscuits, and great slabs of rich black fruit cake, always made months ahead and left to ripen in its tin. By the time it was ready to serve, it would have absorbed the best part of its chief flavouring – a bottle of Bourbon.

To return from this gastronomic digression to the question of place, the other pole (from the downtown) of Lexington life was what we always called the 'horse farms'. Why did we avoid calling a stud a stud? The American language seems to have an innate drive to euphemism, so let me state the fact clearly: there was no industry at all in Lexington when I was a boy. Apart from the growing of tobacco, it had an economy dependent entirely on the copulations of Thoroughbred horses. I was not shown the breeding sheds when I was a child.

No wonder. With its paraphernalia of special stalls to keep expensive but inexperienced mares still so they won't do themselves a damage, devices to tie their tails back out of the way of the stallion's advancing member, and special but suggestive vocabulary for these such as 'twitcher', and the 'teaser' who excites the mare for the stallion, but is never allowed to mate with her, the Thoroughbred horse breeding establishments of Lexington give lessons in sex education few parents would wish their children to have. I only learnt the colourful details of the business when I was over forty and the *Observer* Magazine sent me back to Lexington to prepare a feature in anticipation of the Queen's first visit there.

The beauty of almost every one of these knocking shops for Thoroughbreds adequately cloaks the more sordid side of the town's main source of revenue, which also assures the maintenance of high property values. As I discovered on my 1984 visit, those values are now so high per acre that only existing millionaires and Arab princelings can afford to buy any of them. Who wouldn't, if he had the money, invest in these rolling meadows whose grass, it is claimed, glints blue in the sun? Who would begrudge a few tens of thousands a year to paint all the barns red and all the wooden fences white, as actually happens at Calumet Farm, the prettiest of them all? Who would not pay almost anything to live in the Greek-pillared high-ceilinged antebellum mansions most of the farms boast – even if some of them were built fairly recently?

We were all affected by our proximity to so much horseflesh. As soon as I was tall enough to sit on a horse, I was taken for weekly riding lessons to Cobb Ryan's riding academy. I have probably mis-spelled Cobb Ryan's name, for he was not Irish but Danish. The riding school was opposite Calumet farm, tucked in behind the airport, and reached by the road to Blue Grass Field, as the single runway airfield was called. There was so little commercial air traffic then that there was virtually no problem of horses being spooked by the aeroplanes. In any case, Cobb Ryan's nags were mostly too old and too disciplined to take any notice. We rode English, not western style, of course, and were expected to turn up for lessons in jodhpurs or breeches, not jeans. Oddly enough, we were not made to wear hats, and hard shoes were as acceptable as boots, though you had to carry a proper riding crop. I adored my riding lessons, and the yearly shows in which everyone got a prize.

My greatest triumph was the day I took my first jump. I was exhilarated — completely unfrightened and almost surprised at how brave I was. I have never since been nervous of any horse — which turned out to be foolish fairly recently when I rode a Lippizaner stallion that ran away with me over the plains of central Hungary. My seat may not win prizes in equestrian events, but thanks to Cobb Ryan it remains firm. Though a deal of skin was removed from my bottom and the insides of my thighs and calves were terminally chafed, I was still on the horse when he finally returned me to the Magyar groom who had so incautiously sent us for our unaccompanied gallop.

As horse-mad as any pubescent girl, I lived for my weekly riding lessons, and dreamed of owning my own horse. I should have delighted in grooming it, caring for the tack, and even mucking out its stable. And why not? We had our own paddocks and barns, for heaven's sake — one horse would have gone unnoticed on any of our farms. But Murph wouldn't hear of it. He scoffed at my saying I'd look after the horse myself. I suppose he was right, in that I could never have got to the farm as often as once a day — if there hadn't been a car pool arrangement, my parents would have found it impossible to allow me to have riding lessons. (In fact, I think my lessons may well have been a gift from Lil; perhaps she was also responsible for my transport.) Murph always regretted that I did not take more of an interest in the farms; he missed a trick when he didn't let me have my own horse.

Also opposite the airport on the other side of the Versailles Road is the exquisitely beautiful Keenland race course. We all loved going to the races — especially with Tootsie, who invariably picked a winner. (She often fibbed, perhaps from superstition, about which horse she was backing. More than once she sent me to the Tote window to place a decoy minimum $2 bet for her, while she nipped around to another window and placed her real and much larger bet.)

Keenland held a dangerous attraction for my brother Sandy. I can't think how he could have been allowed through the entrance gate when he was so obviously a child – and a tiny one at that. I suppose they were so used to the sight of the jockeys that they saw no correlation between height and age. Not long after Murph and Shirley had warned him with menaces to stay away from the track (and not to use the bookmaking services of the black locker-room attendants at Shirley's golf club), he was caught in the act. A photograph of him exultantly clutching a winning daily double ticket appeared on the society page of the local newspaper.

A little light industry now exists in Lexington. It received its greatest boost in this direction when I was twelve or thirteen, and IBM decided to build a plant there to assemble electric typewriters – so we were told. Probably it evolved into something to do with computers. The influx of population created by the location of IBM included a large number of affluent, educated, but unalterably northern, Jews, which very much changed the character of the town for us indigenes.

But the important and socially prominent people in the town continue to be, as they were in my day, the bearers of familiar and famous names. There are the socialites, Sonny and Marylou Whitney. He is something to do with Pan American Airlines, but the name was made known in racing circles by John Hay Whitney, sometime Ambassador to the Court of St James and publisher of the *International Herald Tribune*. I made a new friend when my paper sent me to my hometown. John Gaines is the heir to a pet food fortune; he assembled the best collection of drawings in private hands apart from that of H.M. the Queen, including masterpieces of works on paper from Dürer to Picasso, and increased his fortune by $21,288,300 when he sold them at Sotheby's in November 1986. Gainesway Farm has stallions to stud who command fees of hundreds of thousands of dollars; John lives stylishly but not immodestly on the property in a handsome farmhouse furnished with choice *meubles* and the odd Giambologna sculpture of a horse – to remind him what it's all about. His drawings were housed in the National Gallery, and he had transparencies of them stuck up on the glass patio door where he kept his exercise bicycle, so he could see them as he pedalled. Perhaps he decided the trannies were adequate. In Lexington, John Gaines is keen on helping several local Roman Catholic charities. I seldom see him, but when I do we always swap the names and addresses of the newest restaurants in New York and London. John loves entertaining in restaurants, though he is vegetarian.

I renewed an old acquaintance on that trip, too, one who had known me, anyway, since I was small. George Price Headley's cousin Martha Johnston, was for many years our next door neighbour but one; and her three children were close to me in age. (The eldest, Tom, I met again recently when his French wife, Mireille, the author of two admirable cookery books, introduced herself to Jane Grigson and me after we had given a press conference in Paris – for what reason I can't remember. Tom is a film maker, and lives in the flat with the best views in Paris, passed along to him by Pierre Salinger, with whom he worked on the Bobby Kennedy presidential campaign.) George had created a private museum on his small stud, in which were competently displayed bibelots wrought in precious and semi-precious gems and metals.

Some of these George had commissioned, mostly from jewellers, others he had actually designed if not made himself: he had trained as an artist in Paris. Many of the objects included a movement. I was particularly struck by his piece in homage to the first moon landing, in which the bejewelled gold astronaut emerges from his nacreous spacecraft on to a gold moon whose craters are marked by rubies and diamonds; he, and it, were orbited by the enamelled globe of earth, the seas green and the continents picked out in different coloured gems. There were many things in this vein, some silly, most beautiful and all ingenious; there was a smattering of antique objects, and some that incorporated an antiquity, such as a classical coin or medal, in their design.

George really loved these exquisite toys, and had engaged a serious designer to light them and arrange their display. There were two other buildings in the museum. One held oriental costumes and artifacts that, I think he told me, had been collected by past generations of his family.

The other was a grotto constructed entirely of shells. It was awfully kitsch at first sight, but I grew fond of it on subsequent visits. George said that it was a particular favourite of Princess Margaret. He was blasé about the royal family, as his guest book recorded a startling number of visits from members of the Windsor family. At the time he showed me his book, though, he was uneasy about whether his museum was to be included on the forthcoming royal itinerary, as he was anxious to add 'Elizabeth R' to his autograph collection; and he confided to me that he had written a note or two to the Palace as well as dropping a friendly hint to H.M.'s Lexington hosts.

On my second or third visit, George invited me – and my *Observer* photographer – to his house, a few steps across the garden from the museum buildings. It was a simple, neo-Georgian house, with southern variations, like several of the houses Uncle Louis and Aunt Lil had owned. Except for the swimming pool, which flowed through a grotto, to become a small pond fed by a fountain on the patio reached by exiting the house through George's 'den'. This latter room was distinguished by the odd objects that were suspended from the ceiling: memory says there were stuffed birds and a heavy weapon of some sort. Adjacent to the den was the formal drawing room, crammed with paintings, sculptures, porcelain and furniture, much of it of museum quality – and not just by the standards of his own. This was the house where George had lived with his late wife, who was a Whitney. (Between the two of them they were related to almost every name of consequence in the Thoroughbred breeding establishment, including Hal Price Headley and Ben Ali Haggar – after whom the local cinema, the Ben Ali theatre, was called.) George then lived there alone, attended by his black housekeeper, to whom he was no trouble as, he told me, he ate only breakfast cereals and fresh blueberries.

His diet may have been connected with religion. For he suddenly asked us if we'd like to photograph him in his new Thai Buddhist monk's robes. Minutes later he appeared draped in saffron. He was, he assured me, entitled to the uniform. He'd spent several months in a monastery in Thailand and was a fully qualified Buddhist monk. He was sincere, but there was also mischief in his eyes. My photographer and I agreed later that for George, entering a monastery was a gesture of coming out. When we parted this time, George commissioned me to order a clutch of ties for him from his Jermyn Street shirtmaker (and snipped off a little bit of the silk of each of the ties he wanted copied) and invited me and my family to stay in his guest house the next time we were in Lexington. I had every intention of accepting and was doubly saddened to learn that he had died before we could do so. And a little shocked. He had said he wasn't perfectly well, but he was so obviously enjoying his life and a sort of freedom that he had wrested from it by his own struggles. I hope the museum has survived George's death.

The Gainses, the Whitneys, the Headleys, Warren and Bertha Wright at Calumet – and a dozen or so others – were the aristocracy of Lexington, the top rank of the civilisation founded on equine coupling. We didn't see a great deal of any of them when I was a child. Partly this was because many of them had second homes in Saratoga, New York (where Marylou Whitney continues to give lavish parties such as the recent one where she made her entrance dressed in white on a sledge pulled by a white horse) and apartments in Manhattan. It would have been a foolish parent who allowed his child to be educated in the Lexington or Fayette County school system when such superior alternatives as New York or Saratoga were available; and most of their kids were educated privately in the east anyway. So there was little reason for anyone of my generation to meet any of our pre-jet-set aristos (though I did meet those of their children who were educated locally – at a remarkable southern institution called the Cotillion, of which more later).

There was another reason, though, why my parents wouldn't have known most of these people socially. 'Society' met and held its dances and dinners at that quintessentially suburban institution mis-named the 'country club' and, in Lexington, membership in the two most socially desirable of these was 'restricted'. That is, Jews were not welcome as members. There was no objection to a member bringing an occasional Jewish guest to the Lexington Country Club, especially to a big party; but I do not ever remember setting foot inside the Idle Hour Country Club. The latter was exactly opposite no fewer than three of Lil's houses; and grand and rich though she was in her hey-day, I do not think she was more than once or twice inside the precincts of the Idle Hour.

It was worse than unfortunate – it was inconvenient; for she was a keen golfer and they had an excellent course. Jewish golfers had to drive ten miles or so to Boiling Springs Country Club, or play, humiliatingly, on the public links at Picadome. Mind you, if there had been a large enough Jewish population, the Jews of Lexington would have done the same as those of Louisville and Cincinnati and set up an all-Jewish club from which they would with relish have excluded their lower-caste co-religionists.

Almost everyone who has ever addressed himself to the subject, from Toqueville to Mrs Trollope to more recent American academic sociologists, has claimed that social class,

70

as such, doesn't exist in America. They never lived in Lexington.

Class distinctions have now been codified. There is a 'Blue Book' published, with the names and addresses given, of everyone anyone in it could possibly wish to write to or telephone. It is a thin volume. It includes a list of the current year's débutantes. (I kid you not; the Season was instituted in Lexington twenty-odd years ago, not all that long after the abolition of the ceremony of presenting the new crop of British débutantes at Court.) The new, more formal, social arrangements mean that Jews are no longer excluded (my niece, whose name is Jennifer Levy, was a débutante in 1985, which was very jolly for everybody except her father, who had to foot some substantial bills); the absence of Jewish surnames from a printed list would be too unsubtle for words. And now the rising bourgeoisie, who is knocking at the door of the Idle Hour, is really menacing; for the doctors, lawyers and bankers who want in (though not, of course, publically) are black.

Eventually, even the barriers erected by the private clubs will fall, just as the Jim Crow laws were voided and the schools desegregated. But these last walls, those of social class, will leave a cowering, terrified élite exposed when they are breached. For, as any competent culture anthropologist will tell you, these are the demarcations of the marriage groups. In my parents' time, it was unthinkable for a Jew to marry 'out'; the pressures on my generation were not so strong, and being Jewish was no obstacle to my being included in the social events of the upper and middle classes that defined the pool of available marriage partners (though as we got older and past puberty, we were 'weeded', until I was one of only two or three eligible Jewish kids in Cotillion). The only thing expected of my niece is that she will marry one of her dancing partners (or his equivalent); her Jewish descent is irrelevant.

Chapter Five

It would be appropriate if, like Proust's hero, my first memory was a taste or a smell. But the first thing I can remember is being sexually molested by my black mammy. She was called Sally, and it happened while she was sitting on the edge of the bath. She was slim, pretty and young, nothing at all like the rest of the succession of black women who brought me up. Sally had just bathed me and dried me. She tweaked my penis (I can't recall the children's name for the male organ that we used in our family, though I'm sure we had one, as we did for the other interesting bits of the anatomy and for those bodily functions that particularly fascinate children), lifted her skirts and placed my three- or four-year-old body between her legs. I don't remember whether she was wearing knickers, and I don't remember whether I enjoyed it.

My memory of this event is entirely visual; and I was stunned, only a few years ago, to see a painting by an American artist exhibited in a London Gallery that depicted exactly the same scene – or the prelude to it. In the picture, as in life, the little boy was blond, the pretty maid black. My psychoanalyst made the natural assumption, when we discussed this twenty years or so after it happened, that I must have been frightened; and that, at the least, it must have been an unpleasant experience. I'm not sure he was correct. I have neutral feelings about it now, but it seems quite likely to me that I *did* enjoy it. Since becoming a father myself, I'm convinced that most children's interest in sex is bounded only by their mercifully short attention spans.

After I was grown up I once asked my mother about Sally. She was a little surprised to be told why I was curious, but confirmed that I remembered correctly the name of the girl, the address we were living at then, and some of the details of the apartment. It was on Cochran Road.

Of our brief time in the flat on Cochran Road, where I was taken following my birth in the Good Samaritan Hospital, I remember only two things: the bath-time episode with Sally and the exquisite pleasure of peeling strips of wallpaper off the wall of my nursery. The paper was printed with pictures of characters from Mother Goose rhymes, and I could reach the loose edge of one of the seams by standing in my cot.

I have always relished my social life, and was born to be a party-giver – or so my mother tells me. Soon we moved to a semi-detached house in Sherman Avenue, where I began my career as a host. Shirley had just bathed me. Still naked I darted into the living room where she and I had been listening to the radio. (Circumstances convince me it was Saturday night, so perhaps we had just heard the latest instalment of 'Mr Keen, Tracer of Lost Persons' or 'The Creaking Door, Tales of Mystery, Designed to Keep You in . . . Sus-pense'.) We had been nibbling something – crisps or the peanuts we now know (but didn't then) you mustn't give to children.

Next door (we shared a front entrance) they were having a dinner party. While Shirley was still cleaning the bath, I was handing 'round the crisps or nuts to next door's guests, who didn't seem to find anything odd in being served by a naked four-year-old. As I had often done the same thing at home with parental encouragement, Shirley's blushes on this occasion puzzled me. It was difficult to see what I had done that was incorrect. It never occurred to me that the fault lay not in my behaviour but in my lack of clothes.

We always lived as close as possible to Lil and Tootsie;

Shirley and Lil must have shopped for houses in pairs. This time, they were just through the back garden gate, though the streets we lived on were worlds apart. I don't know whether Sherman Avenue was already a bit seedy when we lived there, but eight years later, when I was at Kenwick School just around the corner, it was definitely on the wrong side of the tracks. Uncle Louis, Lola (I think it is time for me to revert to my childish name for this important character in my story) and Tootsie, on the other hand, lived in high bourgeois splendour just fifty steps away on Fairway Drive, across the social gulf of the garden gate. Their house was airy and light, our 'duplex' pinched and mean.

On the other hand, their house was crowded. Ours contained only Shirley, Sandy (though I have absolutely no recollection of him at this time) and me, for it was early 1945 and Murph was still working in the Defence Plant that allowed him to be a respectable draft dodger. Perhaps his mother or father had put some pressure on their only son to stay out of the army. That seems unlikely, as by 1943 at the very latest, every Jew in the world knew that this war was his personal fight. I know, because he told me, that Murph found his cadet corps (ROTC) training at university extremely disagreeable. He did everything he could to avoid military service, starting with fathering me. Married men with children were called up only after single and childless men. His health wasn't brilliant: he suffered a lot from bursitis, and very soon after the war had an operation to remove a calcium deposit from the cheek of his face.

Even so, I find it hard to understand Murph's reluctance to fight. He revered Roosevelt, for whom he'd voted in every election, who was leading America into battle – against Hitler, for heaven's sake, whom he must have known was responsible for murdering whatever was left in Europe of his mother's and father's families. No one has ever suggested to me that Murph was a coward, but I am not sure that I have not reached that conclusion myself. I regret I never asked him about this directly.

Indirectly, I did know a bit about his attitudes. This was because I was in danger of being drafted myself, when I officially graduated from university in the early summer of 1963. I had extremely strong and, I thought (and still do) principled reasons for wishing to avoid the draft. Though Murph was horrified by the bright red colour of my political views, he could see, not my objections to the war in Vietnam that was just starting, but the likelihood of me being sent there if I was drafted. Someone on the local draft board was gunning for me – or more likely, had a grudge against Murph – for, strictly speaking, it wasn't my turn to be called up. But I was. I got out of it in a very droll manner, which I shall explain later. My cohort, the unfortunate group of less privileged boys whom I would have joined, was sent to the 101st Airborne Division, at Fort Campbell, Kentucky, for their basic training, and thence to Vietnam. I have never been so sorry to have been proved right.

Apart from listening endlessly to the radio with my mother, I have virtually no memories of life at Sherman Avenue. The radio was contained in one of those enormous floor-standing consoles. It incorporated a gramophone, and we had a large collection of records; but my consciousness of those was, I think, formed in our next house. For the moment it was all: 'Lamont Cranston, wealthy man about town, has another identity, in which he fights crime: The Shadow. Who knows what evil lurks in the heart of man? The Shadow knows!' and 'Drinkin' beer in a cabaret, and was I havin' fun;/ and then one night/ she caught me right,/ and now I'm on the run', which is the first verse of the forties pop song, whose chorus is 'Lay that pistol down, babe,/ oh, lay that pistol down!/ Pistol-packin' Mama,/ oh, lay that pistol down!' My mother had nothing to do but to teach me to read. I had nothing to do but to learn. I had a prodigious memory.

What I can't remember is the birth of my younger brother. That was in the spring of 1944, April 10th. As any psycho-analyst will tell you (and has told me often enough), it must have been such a traumatic event for me that I shut it out of my conscious memory. And my unconscious, too, come to that: when I was a child and even when I was a young man in analysis, I never dreamt of my brother. In my dreams I still often return to various childhood haunts and abodes – most usually our subsequent house, or my grandparent's house, or the two of Uncle Louis's and Lil's that I especially loved; but in these dreams I am an only child. My brother has been getting even for it ever since.

This is perhaps the place to say that our parents played the unwitting name trick on my brother as well. I have no idea whose Hebrew name he bears. Though I don't remember it (and I doubt that there is anyone alive who does), I should guess from the version *anglice* that it is something like 'Shmuel Eliyahu', or Samuel Elijah, both names that a person of character would relish. My poor brother was condemned to another of those made-up would-be Anglo-Saxon names, Sanford Eliot. He has always been known as 'Sandy'. As he has inherited the family diminutiveness and is less than five foot two, it seems unfair to have reinforced Nature by calling him by an intractably diminutive name.

The existence of my brother entered my consciousness only after we moved house. This we must have done as soon as the war was over and Murph came home. Our new address was 761 Cooper Drive, and it was my favourite of all the houses in which we lived. It was probably brand new when Murph bought it, but it had generous rooms, of which I can remember three on the ground floor: a kitchen, with a walk-through pantry connecting it to the dining room, and a living room, through which you entered a large, screened-in verandah. I am vague about the upstairs.

There was a large front lawn, with the usual concrete path

bisecting it, and on its southern border a long drive ran downhill to a free-standing garage. The slope was quite steep; you had to walk down quite a substantial wooden staircase to get to the back garden. And what a wonderful garden it was. Eden-like, it had scented roses in the summer, lilac and tulips in spring, and even a trumpet vine, *Bignonia*, that had humming-birds feeding in its bells. That grew at the back of the garage. Then there was a gentle hill (but steep enough to roll down and excellent for children's games), and a flat lawn that ended in a screen of hedges. Thanks to Uncle Louis, the lawn had a large Wendy house on its south side. Beyond the hedges, to the west, was a flimsy wire fence, all that separated us from the pond of the neighbouring farm.

That pond was a source of wonder – and of horror. Once a pig had her litter on its banks – and then devoured them before our terror-filled eyes. I never had any trouble understanding what James Joyce meant about Ireland being 'the sow that eats her farrow'. And the pond brought the serpent into our Eden, for we knew it contained the venomous snake called the Water Moccasin. We never actually saw one of those, but once, when Tootsie was left in charge of us, she showed more brute strength than I thought her capable of and dispatched a perfectly harmless Garter snake with the business end of a spade. Any snake, after all, might have been the dreaded viper we knew we nourished at only one remove from our bosom.

The front garden had its pleasures too. The path in the middle was a perfect dividing line for games such as Red Rover. At dusk on a balmy spring or early summer evening, after supper and just before the fireflies began their luminous winking, the neighbourhood children would gather. Several of them had names wonderfully evocative of old Dixie: Hunter Isaacs, Retta Johnston, Woody Simpson, Boo Wyman. We'd divide into two teams, and each would hold hands to form a human chain on either side of the path. Then the (probably self-appointed) captain of the side whose turn it was would chant, 'Red Rover, Red Rover, we dare PAUL to come over!' and you would loose yourself from your team-mates' grasp and launch yourself at the opposing side. Victory was achieved by breaking through their lines.

The rules were simple, easy to follow and the game provided comradeship. Some of us needed that. Several of our parents were in the throes of splitting up, mine included. It was considered a treat for us to be allowed to play after supper; but more than once we were encouraged to gather some friends in the 'front yard' to disguise the sound of raised voices.

Shirley and Murph never shouted at each other or even quarrelled in front of us. Considerate though this may have been, perhaps it was a little less than wise, for it left us unprepared for what was to come. I was totally surprised when Murph moved out of Cooper Drive and went back to live with his parents. It was all explained to us in what was then a most progressive and civilised manner, and each made an effort not to be rude or even unkind about the other to the children. It was bewildering. Nothing appeared to be wrong. Why did our father have to live somewhere else?

I was six; Sandy was three. It may well have been worse for him. Perhaps he sensed that his very existence was a failure: I later learnt that the marriage had been in trouble for years and years, and Sandy was conceived in the hope that another baby would improve matters.

This was a time in my childhood beloved of my shrink. (This must be the place to reveal that he was called Dr Kavka – true, I promise you; only the spelling distinguished him from the almost certainly related Franz.) An orthodox Freudian, he naturally saw this period as my Oedipal crux, and insisted that if I only tried I could recall my sense of jubilation at having so prevailed over my father in the struggle for my mother's affections that he left the house in defeat. Try as I might, I found it difficult to remember these feelings of victory. But I got the point. He was saying that I found it difficult to accept success, because I felt so guilty over my first and greatest triumph.

Murph and Shirley were divorced in 1947. Funnily enough, most of my recollections of life at Cooper Drive are pleasant ones. I do remember being a bit disturbed when Shirley's brother Manuel came to live with us for a time. Not by his presence, though; if anything, I hero-worshipped him. He was only just recently out of uniform and had gone back to college, where his enviable life seemed to me to consist of dance bands, football games, fraternity meetings and dates with girls, all of whom I addressed as Rosemary, the only one whose name I could remember.

There was, however, a dark side to our relationship. One day he came home with two pairs of boxing gloves: he had decided we needed lessons in the manly art. (In fact, he probably thought subconsciously that we just needed some lessons in being male – and he was, I'm sure now, right.) We each in turn put on the gloves and squared off with 'Unc'. (I'm not sure how one would spell the diminutive by which we called him.) Three-year-old Sandy was dusted lightly with the tips of the gloves, but I got a pounding.

It surprised me. I wasn't used to being hit. My father once took his belt to me for being cheeky to Shirley; however, that was one of the few instances of corporal punishment I can recollect. Shirley, it is true, had a terrible and frightening temper, but lost it rarely. I don't think I ever fell victim to it physically, although Sandy did: she once got so angry with him that she dislocated his arm by yanking him up from the floor where he stubbornly insisted on remaining. But not me; never me. I was either too good or too canny to merit even the perfectly normal quota of parental smacks. I wonder, though, whether I got many cuddles.

By this time, aged six, I was a fat boy. I had already begun to think of myself as unattractive. At four I had my tonsils removed: the operation was then as fashionable and as universal as was circumcision. I never forgot the bribe I was offered to be a good patient: when I woke up after the operation I would be allowed unlimited ice cream – as much as I liked to eat. What I was not told was that my throat would be so sore that, when the ice cream came, I couldn't swallow it. That was my first example of the treachery of grown-ups.

In my childish heart I was certain that they had known when the promise was made that I shouldn't want the ice cream: I felt that my trust had been betrayed. Worse, as soon as I was able to eat again I began to put on weight. I remained a fat and, I felt, unlovable child, until I was twelve. There was a photograph album of pictures of me and my cousin Paul taken in Cleveland when we were three. They showed a handsome, blond, thin little chap (you could be certain of that, as I was nude in several of them). I used to pore over these pictures, envying the little boy in them, but, perversely, feeling alienated from him. Sometimes I thought he was someone else.

My image of myself and my body, however, was not quite correct. The newspaper photograph of Uncle Louis and me was taken when I was nearly six and one-half, and unless I was holding my tummy in for the camera, I was scarcely even plump. I certainly did put on weight – and inches – later, but I doubt if I was ever as repulsively fat as I was in my own mind. Was my obesity of organic or psychological origin? I don't know; but I do know that my entire generation, at least of middle-class kids from affluent households, were taught rotten eating habits. We were forced, because there was a war being fought, to clean our plates, to 'think of all the starving children in China'. I knew perfectly well by the age of four that there was no way to transport any of the food on my plate to China; but that didn't keep me from acquiring the life-long habit of finishing what is set in front of me. The *Observer* once sent me to a Harley Street hypnotist in the course of writing an article about methods of slimming. One of the precepts he tried to din into my mesmerised brain was 'Don't treat your own stomach as if it were somebody else's dustbin.' If only I had encountered the wise Dr Carpenter in my childhood.

There was a memorable variation on this theme a couple of years later when I was seven or eight. Murph had taken Sandy and me to Florida, I suppose during the winter months. There was certainly someone else in our party – probably Murph's elder sister Jenny, for I remember her nursing me through one of my regular, truly terrible cases of sunburn acquired on one of the beaches of Miami. We were in a grand, elegant restaurant that specialised in fish and shellfish, and the two little boys were kitted out in jackets and ties. When the waiter asked what I wanted, Murph said I could order for myself. Knowing brat that I was, I politely said I'd have a lobster. This was partly to impress Aunt Jenny (or whoever our dining companion was). The waiter approved my choice. He had an excellent 'small Florida lobster'.

'Perfect,' said Murph, 'the tail meat will just do for one hungry boy.' He'd made a mistake. All unwitting, my father had strayed onto his son's territory. I knew the difference between the true Maine lobster, *Homarus americanus*, and *Panulirus*, the spiny or rock lobster, really a marine crayfish, found in the warm Florida waters. 'I want one with claws,' demanded the ghastly child. Exasperated, but probably a little proud of his gastronomic prodigy, Murph tried to reason with me. Maine lobsters were bigger than Florida lobsters, too much even for one small but fat boy; Maine lobsters were fiddly to eat; Florida lobsters were just as good.

I countered each and every argument. The waiter was amazed, and Aunt Jenny, if it was she, no doubt conceived her life-long belief that I was a sybarite, liable to squander the family fortunes on edible delicacies. 'I have eaten a Maine lobster before; the quantity was manageable, and so was the anatomy,' and the clincher: '*Everybody* knows Maine lobsters are better than Florida lobsters. And Florida lobsters are not real lobsters anyway.'

With that Murph lost his temper. 'Have you got Maine lobsters?' he asked the patient but bemused waiter. 'Certainly, sir.' 'Then bring the boy the largest one in the kitchen.' The waiter entered willingly into the plot, and brought a meat platter overlapped by what must have been a two-and-a-half pound crustacean.

With bib, nutcrackers, lobster pick and melted butter I set to work, feeling smug and satisfied with my victory. I cracked a claw; I got the meat out almost intact. I was doing what I did best. I crowed my pleasure. Magnanimous in triumph, I offered shares in my lobster to the others at the table. 'No,' said Murph, too firmly, 'eat it all yourself.'

Defeat, when it came, was ignominious. The one claw, and a bite or two of the tail. I could not eat another mouthful for love, money or self-esteem. 'We are in Florida,' said Murph, 'a thousand miles from Maine. Not surprisingly, Maine lobster costs four times as much as Florida lobster. You have just wasted more money than you'll see again until you're grown up. It will have been worth it if you learn the lesson that your eyes are bigger than your stomach.' He didn't rub in the point that my head was bigger than either.

Soon after her divorce, my mother went out to work. I don't know whether this was an economic necessity, or a cure for boredom. In my recollection, all my mother ever did was teach me to read, while we were, for some reason, seated in the pantry between the kitchen and dining room. I do recall that I once reduced her to despair, by pasting all the ration stamps into the book – which I supposed deprived us of some necessaries for a week or so. And I remember discovering electricity. We had a visitor, in full naval whites; he was the black-sheep of the first family of one of Murph's brothers-in-law. I took the opportunity of the distraction created by his presence to find out what would happen if I inserted one of Shirley's hairpins into the wall socket. Fortunately American voltage is only 120, and I survived the all too literal shock.

We still employed a maid – if only to cook, which has never been Shirley's strongest point. Shirley had had to pretend to keep a kosher house. In the first place, she didn't know the rules; in the second, she didn't give a damn. Didn't Murph invariably order ham when we went out to our favourite 'roadhouse' restaurant, the Little Inn? So when my grandmother came around to Cooper Drive to inspect the cupboards, I am afraid she was giving genuine grounds for divorce.

Comically enough, I remember being told that another cause of marital discord was culinary. Ada Gail was famous for her pickled dill cucumbers (justifiably so; she once gave me the recipe, I published it first in the *Observer*, then in the best-selling *Official Foodie Handbook*, and then Time-Life bought it for their volume of *The Good Cook* on pickles and preserves; and the article containing the recipe has been reprinted so often I've lost count). Every summer when Ada made her pickles, she gave us a jar of them. Shirley confessed to me that she had provoked a terrible row by eating all of them at a sitting once while Murph was out of town.

Without any business training, or any experience save that she'd had years earlier at the jewellery shop, Shirley was taken on as a buyer of children's clothes, about which she knew next to nothing, by Maurice and Evelyn Hymson at their chic downtown shop, Tots and Teens. They were doing a good deed. The social stigma of divorce at that time was as great as the shame of having an illegitimate child; and they were good and brave to take on a woman who, in the opinion of most, was no better than she ought to be. Shirley, made tough by the injustice of it all, rewarded the Hymson's kindness by doing the job supremely well. I think everybody concerned was surprised.

Now Rhoda entered my life. Maybe she'd been with us at Cooper Drive all along, but it's at the point when Shirley went to work that I became aware of being utterly dependent on this huge woman who was, in everything but name (because, despite the universal racism of the time and place, it was thought old-fashioned and insulting), my black mammy.

When answering the telephone, Rhoda would identify herself in a drawl so thick that it was really a separate dialect, by saying, 'This is the maid speaking.' But mammy is what Rhoda was, and maid of all work, too. With all the pride of a Norland nanny, she wore a uniform supplied by my mother. Was it a black and white dress of heavy cotton? I can remember little except that it was always covered with a clean apron. Rhoda fed us, bathed us, washed and ironed our clothes, walked me to school and, when we were bad, administered discipline. It was perfectly common for southern kids like us to be brought up by black women, and normal for them, and not the parents, to smack the bottoms of naughty children. It had the advantage enjoyed by nanny-employing Victorians of making the children take a rosy view of their mother. As was the case then, Shirley was nearly always affectionate and always glad to see us. Why not? When presented to her we were clean, tidy, well fed and glad to see her: Rhoda saw to the first three. It was a good arrangement; we all profited.

Shirley sent me to nursery school when I was four or five. There we were given our mid-day meals. I remember being allowed – or perhaps even encouraged – to compose faces of mashed potato, cooked carrots and peas on our plates, on the grounds it would make us more eager to eat up our vegetables. (I was reminded forcefully of my nursery school tucker by a cookery book written in unseemly haste by Barbara Cartland. The plate shots of food that served as its illustrations, and which, she insisted, she had supervised herself, were the most grotesque uses to which I had ever seen food put since then.) After lunch we lay down on a covering on the floor and pretended to have a nap. When the elderly spinster or widow who was supposed to be minding us went off for her cup of tea or her fag, we innocents gave each other our first lessons in sex

84

education. My most vivid memory of nursery school is olfactory; I can still smell the whiff of disinfectant combined with that of cooked carrots and canned peas.

Nursery school was a little difficult for me, as the children weren't supposed to be able to read, which I was able to do with fluency by the end of the year or two in which I was an inmate. The same was true of kindergarten; we weren't allowed to start school proper until age six; if my birthday had been before January, I should have slipped in under the wire; but it was late February, and I was condemned to march with my own cohort. (Later, when Shirley was advised that I ought to 'skip a grade' of primary school, she refused; the prevailing educational orthodoxy said it was better for a child to remain with his own age group. Too bad; I was awfully bored.)

It was a great relief when I was finally eligible to start the first grade at M. A. Cassidy Elementary School. 'Miz Miller' (could that have been her name? We southerners had developed the universal female title that does not reveal marital status generations before anyone ever thought of the ridiculous 'Ms') could really *teach* me something now, such as how to write in joined-up letters (a skill the mastery of which took me more years than this one), and how to do sums. At the beginning of our careers we were given a sort of general knowledge quiz, I suppose because tyro schoolchildren, having no records, have never been assessed and beget no expectations – which makes teacher's job tough. It was nothing extraordinary to be the cleverest child in a group of thirty children all brought up in one small town; but Miz Miller had the grace to profess herself astonished when I answered one of the quiz questions that had to do with identifying a popular singer by the sound of his recorded voice. (If it wasn't Tony Martin, it was Mel Tormé.) Miz Miller was not yet aware of my radio addiction. She made no bones about my being teacher's pet, a position I confidently expected to occupy forever.

I was not the only kid who was brought to school by a black lady. This merely denoted a child of the middle-classes; it was not even necessary to have a working mother to qualify. I don't know for how long Rhoda was obliged to be the 1940s' pedestrian equivalent of the school run, but we were less than a mile away, and as soon as I could be trusted not to be foolish about crossing roads, I was allowed to go to and from school by myself.

We travelled, of course, in a pack, picking up and dropping off children who lived along the route. That was until one day when I persuaded Woody Simpson, an attractive character who (I think) was one of Henry Clay's seemingly rare non-black and non-Jewish descendants, to take a 'short cut' home via the back gardens of half the streets in an arc with a one-mile radius of my house. I was several hours late getting home, where I was confronted by a furious Shirley, who had been summoned home from work by a distraught Rhoda. When I explained that I was so late because I had taken a short cut, Shirley suspended the no-smacking rule and gave me a quite painful geometry lesson. I never again forgot that the shortest distance between two points is a straight line.

Apart from this, Shirley's views with regard to discipline were that children did not require to be punished for breaking things unless it was done on purpose. Fortunately I was graceful, as fat children often are; whereas my brother was so clumsy that he appeared to have the opposite effect to Medusa's stare – at a glance from him precious objects would shatter. (There was even a time when he was discouraged from handling Uncle Louis's mechanical banks, and they, remember, were cast iron.) Threats to run away from home were common, but invariably frustrated by Shirley's offering, if we would wait a few moments, to 'pack you all a good lunch and give y'all five dollars', which was a good deal of money then.

Cassidy was a comfortable school, and I was happy. Mrs McGraw, the third grade teacher demonstrated her favouritism when she went on a trip to Washington, D C, and brought back for me, in time for the Independance Day celebrations on July the 4th, a giant cardboard fire-cracker filled with cello-phane-wrapped toffees. I was looking forward to finishing all six grades there, and progressing in the normal way to Morton Junior High School, set in spacious grounds only a few steps to the east, to complete the next three.

Then disaster struck. We moved. This was because Shirley remarried. I didn't mind that – I even quite liked my new step-father – but I was heartbroken at leaving Cooper Drive and my school. And I was right to be apprehensive. My new school was called Picadome, like the golf course.

I hated it on sight. The buildings were old and smelly (if Cassidy had the normal disinfected odour of premises that contain lots of children, I never noticed) and the other children were not like the clean and proper Cassidy kids. The kids at Picadome were rough, mostly lower-middle and working-class kids, I suppose, but with a pungent leaven of rural child-ren. The school's catchment area included a lot of the outlying county. They didn't have hayseeds in their teeth and muddy boots, but they did wear patched dungarees and speak in dialect. And not the cozy black southern speech of Rhoda, but twangy mountain dialect from the east of the state. They were hillbillies, the descendants of the feuding, violent Hatfields and McCoys. It was frightening.

Why had we come down in the world quite so far? I wondered. In fact, my snobbish instincts proved to be correct. The school was dreadful. The teachers, with the single exception of a kind woman whose name I have forgotten, saw their job as keeping the yokels in order rather than inculcating facts – or even good habits. These teachers didn't have pets, only greater and lesser enemies. One of them struck me once; she had no use for an academically apt little boy who must have been troublesome. I complained to my parents, but got no hearing. I expect Murph thought it was character-building;

and he wasn't all that sorry to see me getting a lesson in democracy by making my way with the toughs and the rustics.

Rhoda, of course, came with us when we moved. Some of the boys in our new neighbourhood were a little less genteel than she would have liked, and she made certain they did not mistake the coolness of their welcome for a mere lack of enthusiasm: none of them ever returned a second time, and I was not bullied.

My protector did not live in, but arrived before Shirley went off to work and stayed until after she returned, preparing and sometimes serving the evening meal. At Cooper Drive, Rhoda had also been our babysitter when necessary, and I think stayed in the house when my parents were away. She herself lived in one of the black neighbourhoods in which Uncle Louis owned property.

She did not live alone, but with her 'common-law' husband, a rangy black man of indeterminate age and few teeth called 'Lige', short for Elijah, who often worked for us as a handyman. Though he counted as a family retainer of sorts, I do not think Lige was ever invited to put on a white jacket and mix and serve the drinks at any of our parties. This was the traditional role of the black male domestic help, but Lige's appearance made this impossible – he was just too scruffy. (When we needed a butler-type, we had to borrow Alec or Stanley, who were brothers, from the Meyers family. Alec was dignified and gentlemanly; Stanley was younger and cool, his young and pretty wife, Dovey, worked for us for a while, but was too flighty to be in charge of my brother and me for long.)

Rhoda and Lige took each other very much for granted. But they obviously had some recreations. I know, because they once employed me to buy some marijuana for them. In Lige's old banger we drove to a chemist's shop on Jefferson Street, in a predominantly black area. I was given some money and told to hop out of the car and ask the man behind the counter for some 'reefers', while Rhoda and Lige waited in the car across the road. It was perfectly sensible to use me as a courier. No one could possibly think I wanted the dope for myself, but no one would connect me with the real buyers either. On reflection, I can't imagine the police being interested anyway – they had much bigger fish to fry. Lexington was then the location of the Federal Narcotics Hospital, 'Narco' to the locals. The town was awhirl with more serious drug activity, as there was a thriving business supplying hard drugs to the inmates, such as Billie Holliday and Judy Garland, with their guards serving as the middlemen.

Was Rhoda a good cook? It is extraordinary that I can't remember what she cooked for Shirley and me. I say this, because our household by now practised culinary apartheid, and Rhoda was obliged, for the most part, to prepare separate meals for us and for my brother.

Sandy had always been a fussy eater. He had been indulged in his whimsical diet at first out of an unspoken sympathy for him as the chief victim of the traumata of divorce. 'Poor little mite', was the general view, 'no wonder he's off his food.' One by one my brother eliminated sources of nutrients. First he refused salads, then green vegetables, then all vegetables. Fruit went next. Soon fish, meat and bread became taboo; and just to show that he was both systematic and in earnest, most sweets were banned.

By the time he was aged five, Sandy would eat nothing except southern fried chicken and chocolate. This diet he enforced himself. It was more rigorously observed than Grandmother Levy could ever have obeyed the laws of *kashrut*. Sandy appointed himself the head of the gastro-police, and watched Rhoda fry his batch of chicken every other day: he had no objection to having it cold on the second day. A more serious matter was for him to satisfy himself that no flavouring apart from chocolate made its way into the dessert. All this watchfulness and fastidiousness made him a precocious child.

On the first Christmas we had away from Cooper Drive, a parcel arrived for Sandy from Florida. Though it had arrived a little early, it was obviously a Christmas present from Aunt Kay, who lived in Miami, where you could buy the sophisticated confection the parcel held. Sandy fell upon the package and ripped off its wrappings, heedless of Rhoda's pleadings to save it for Christmas, to reveal a slab of a creamy white substance that was obviously a sweet.

Enraged, Sandy stormed out of the house, through the screened back door, carrying Aunt Kay's offering, paper and all. With a clatter of metal lids, he very audibly flung the lot into the dustbin. We could hear him carrying on a dialogue with himself – through his tears of anger: 'How dare she send me this junk! *Everybody* knows I only eat chocolate.' His dignity was further wounded, and tears, but this time of remorse, appeared again, when Aunt Kay's letter to Shirley was read out the next day: 'I hope Sandy will enjoy the white chocolate; it's the first time they've ever had it in the candy store. I'm sorry I couldn't find anything equally interesting to send to your Paul.'

Sandy's eating habits evolved into a more reasonable diet gradually. It was found that he would eat things other than fried chicken, providing whatever it was was covered or mixed with Hershey's chocolate syrup. Rhoda found it quite easy to get him to drink milk turned brown with this sticky goo, and to get him to eat breakfast cereal. I have a vision of Sandy eating boiled prawns smothered in chocolate sauce; but I think that must have been my private fantasy.

My own culinary education had been begun by Lil's lobster when I was four; it was now to continue under the aegis of my mother's new husband.

Chapter Six

'Babe' Meyers married Shirley in 1949, after having, more or less, asked permission from my brother and me. He courted us, as he had wooed Shirley, with food. At a proper formal dinner he had cooked himself at the bachelor apartment on Second or Third Street he shared with the madcap 'Cokey' Hymson (he was Maurice's younger brother and his proper name is Sheldon), he gave Shirley, Sandy and me avocado pear. How could he have bought an avocado in Lexington in 1948 or 1949? It would have been as easy to find a pheasant or a bottle of Château d'Yquem.

Unfortunately, we didn't know how to eat it. Babe realised that it had to be peeled and, either because he had an intuition or because he'd had a previous encounter with an avocado in Chicago or New York, he served it to us sliced up in a salad. What he didn't know was how to tell when it was ripe; so the first avocado I ever tasted was just a little the wrong side of crunchy.

The second course was likely to have been a curry. Babe had served with the US Army Quartermaster Corps in India. A 'curry' meant meat or chicken stewed up with tinned curry powder (a commodity rarer than avocados), onions, garlic, coconut and probably apple, served with rice, sliced banana, grated desiccated coconut and Major Gray's chutney. From the day I first met Babe, I was under strict orders whenever I left Lexington for a more populous city (there were frequent excursions to Cincinnati or Cleveland), never to come back without a bottle of Major Gray's chutney. Babe taught Rhoda and her successor, Mary Elizabeth, to make this intriguing bastard dish. I never tasted its equivalent until thirty-five years later, when I was served its twin at lunch at *Punch* magazine.

Babe's real name was Arthur. His epithet was easily accounted for: he was the youngest of at least six brothers. They were all, I think, born at Louisville, and each one of them had style and élan. Manuel, who owned Meyers and was one of Murph's closest friends, was one of Babe's elder brothers and, when Babe married Shirley, became my second 'Uncle Manuel'. All the Meyers boys had the same voice, a more sophisticated version of the local drawl. (Manuel had a 'whiskey' voice, gravelly and attractive; I don't think he acquired it from drink, though.) The Meyers men were all snappy dressers; Babe was the first person I ever met who thought clothes were important and interesting. No doubt this was because their father had been a tailor.

Their style was a remarkably accurate version of the clothes worn by an English country gent, the sort of thing Paul Smith and other designers for men call classics; Manny and Babe were actually under the sartorial influence of the Duke of Windsor. They sported soft tweeds, Egyptian cotton shirts, silk paisley ties (or regimental stripes to which they were not entitled and whose significance was not known to them), flannel trousers (or even cavalry twill in winter) and highly polished brogues. This was everyday Lexington wear.

You can take the boy out of Lexington, but you can't take Lexington out of the boy. Babe imparted to me a large number of prejudices about when and where to wear what, and I still cringe when I or another violate any of these law-like precepts. Black shoes only, when in town, is one, as I have confessed, that I sometimes fail to observe. But I live by the rules that one does not wear a white shirt before six o'clock, and that no gentleman wears both a pocket handkerchief and a buttonhole, but one or the other – especially with a dinner jacket. Also that you do not wear a made-up bow tie (though I could never learn to tie my own until I was in my late twenties and was taught to do so very grandly by Lord David Cecil, who had the idea of standing behind me to do the knot, so that I could follow his movements accurately), and that your shoes are always clean and polished, and that you wear braces or a belt but not both. It is a shame that all this sumptuary lore should be wasted on someone like me. I like clothes, but my figure condemns me to involuntary slobbery.

It was just as well for everyone concerned that Uncle Manny was in the business of selling what was required to keep up the particular appearances. Meyers, on West Main Street, where Murph still had the shoe department at the time Manuel's brother became the second husband of his ex-wife, was the most exciting shop I could imagine. Murph's stock of shoes, which was large and valuable, was kept in a series of warrens filled with wooden shelves behind the selling and fitting area, which was at the extreme back of the ground floor of the four-storey building. A few models that were not too much in demand were kept in the basement, a place I loved, as it had the slightly dangerous atmosphere of an under-explored, un-mapped cave.

Most of the ground floor was given over to the display of gentlemen's clothing. It was a riot of tweed, cashmere, silk, cotton and leather. It smelled of expensive leather and aftershave (perhaps the Jamaican Bay Rum Babe used himself; but in my memory's olfactory filing cabinet, I see a note that says it was Caswell & Massey's 'Jockey'). All this was tended, not by ordinary sales assistants, but by family retainers. 'Pete' Hardesty was still advising me on my shirts when he was well in his eighties; the elegant 'J. T.', whose surname I may well never have known, went from youth to middle age in the employ of Meyers; and Frances, the cashier, like Ada Clausen, the book-keeper, must surely have remained on the payroll

93

until death terminated their monthly wages. Dapper black Alec, when he was not being a white-jacketed butler, was in charge of receiving the merchandise: the glorious basement was his domain.

On the first floor was everything required to dress a lady except her shoes. None of this interested me much. I understood that the goods were as fashionable as those to be found in New York or Paris, but at the same prices. There was the cost of getting there to be considered, though. Sometimes the ladies' floor was presided over by Manny's daughter-in-law, a beautiful woman from Pittsburgh with a sophisticated accent and the strange name of Sydelle. Sydelle and Shirley alternated between being bosom friends and deadly enemies, until Shirley and Babe were divorced, and the state of enmity became permanent.

Up one more floor one found the reason for the success of Meyers. The smell of leather was heady here, for the floor held saddles and all the other tack requisite for horsy gentlefolk. English saddles, mind you; we did not tolerate Western vulgarity in Lexington. The Meyers empire was built on a foundation of jodhpurs, breeches and boots; they were the principal riding outfitters to the eastern half of America, a sort of Dixie Moss Bros. This part of the business had been developed by Babe's and Manuel's brother Ed, who had migrated to New York, where he kept us posted on what were the new, hot restaurants and married a brassy blonde Brit as his second wife. Before being bought out by Manny, Ed had, I believe, invented and patented 'Kentucky jodhpurs', a pair of which I still own and occasionally wear to astonish friends who can't believe I can ride.

They are cut tight in the bum, with a flare at the hips, but snug in the calves and thighs, so that there is no material to chafe. This part of the design is mostly traditional, as is the reinforced material on the inside of the thighs; the difference is that they have slightly flared bottoms, with an elastic strap that buttons on either side, so that they will fit over an ordinary shoe, and do not require boots. This makes them easy to get on and off, and very forgiving when on. It's an informal look; the person who sold them to you would have suggested making up a hacking jacket in window-pane or Prince-of-Wales checks to wear with them. Of course, Meyers also did more formal riding wear for shows, and, if you wished, could outfit you as a Master of Foxhounds in the pink.

Babe, sadly for me, had no financial interest in Meyers. This may have been because, as the youngest brother, he would have had very little capital to put up before his Army service. But I think it was more likely that Manuel didn't want him in the business because he wanted to keep its shares intact and undivided for his own son, Marvin, and because he didn't have very much respect for his brother's intellect. Babe, in his turn, regarded his nephew Marvin, of whom he was fond, as more than a little thick.

After the war, no doubt aided by Manuel, Babe set up shop as a dealer in military surplus stocks, in premises bang opposite Meyers. His store was called, accurately and simply enough, Army Goods Headquarters, and he made enough money from it to buy himself a partnership in a really aggressive retail business run by Shirley's Cleveland first cousin Eddy Singer, from which he retired a millionaire. Meyers has since gone bust and disappeared; so I suppose Babe was a better judge of character than Manuel.

As were most of his brothers, Babe, who had obviously once been good-looking, was impressively bald, and like the others, usually had a cigar in his hand or mouth. The whole family was devastated by the aftermath of the Bay of Pigs, in which Havana cigars vanished from the American market.

Another trait shared by all the brothers was that they were connoisseurs and virtuosi of bad language. They all had the ability of the southern-drawling male to stretch 'shee-it', to a third syllable, and their repertory of four-letter words, though not original, was frequently employed. For Babe, swearing was really a verbal tic, a harmless mannerism, at which surprisingly few people took offence. In a fashion I have noticed is peculiar to southerners – and southern men, at that – Babe's speech was punctuated with 'shit', 'fuck', even 'cunt', and frequent 'ass-holes'. 'Goddamn' was only an intensifier; on the whole it replaced 'very' in Babe's vocabulary, and 'hell' did duty for 'indeed', as in 'hell, yes'. The effect was comic; I have seen evangelical Methodist spinster schoolteachers put in a good mood by half an hour's conversation with Babe, and clergymen unable to contain their laughter at his obscene high spirits. He was very lovable.

So was Manuel, except that he had a streak of hauteur, perhaps the result of spending too much time in the company of the aristos to whom he sold his goods. He and Murph were regular travelling companions, so I saw quite a lot of Manny in London. I remember once he was buying vast quantities of old pewter. In an antique shop in Knightsbridge, having already spoken for two or three sets of English graduated measures, he asked to see a set of French measures on a high shelf. It was only a ruse to get the nubile, proto-Sloane Ranger who owned the shop to turn her handsome back to the then seventy-year-old Manny, who, I regret to say, fondled her well-bred bottom.

There was a moment's hesitation, in which the lady debated with herself her course of action. I could see her rapidly doing her sums, mentally adding up the many hundreds of pounds he had spent; she decided against braining the old lecher with the half-litre pot whose handle she was gripping so tightly. Later that week I took Manny to dinner with some wealthy north London Jewish Communist friends (he found the combination unbelievable though Murph, having known the Seifert family for a long time, was quite serene). He challenged his host, a man a little younger than he, to guess his age. When Sigmund Seifert, a solicitor of acutely good judgement of most matters, replied, spot on, 'Seventy', Manny was genuinely cross; and very nearly marched out of the room, saying, 'You son-of-a-bitch. I didn't come here to be insulted.'

Shirley and Babe went on their honeymoon to a resort in Wisconsin that, in 1949, was the *dernier cri*. I know, for Murph had taken us there that year for our summer holidays. We fished mainly. The blue gills were so numerous and hungry for the bait that we caught hundreds. I, not understanding the nature or purpose of our sport, released them from their net prison. When Murph discovered this, he said we'd spend the rest of the afternoon there until we caught the same number again. Then he got the chef to cook the very fish we'd caught and forced me to eat them for supper. I didn't like the idea of eating creatures I had recently met, and sobbed through the meal. I think the point of it was to teach me a lesson about farming; all I really learnt was that fish have nasty bones. We had had to fly via Chicago and Milwaukee to get to this place; it was a fairly early commercial airline flight, being so soon after the war, and I was thrilled by the idea of the aeroplane. Until it took off and I was airsick – for the first and only time. I think Murph's real reason for choosing the place was the governess and dance instructress, Phyllis, whom I suspect he might have known previously. For once we were safely tucked up in bed, I am pretty sure Murph and Phyllis were engaged in more than ballroom dancing lessons.

While Shirley and Babe were on their honeymoon, Sandy and I were lodged, as we frequently were, with Aunt Lola and Uncle Louis, and spent most of the week listening to 'Peter and the Wolf' on the gramophone. I cannot think why, but not only were we excluded from the wedding, we weren't told they were married until they returned from their honeymoon. I suppose they thought we might be upset and spoil the festivities. Come to think of it, we might have done. We were still confused by the divorce, and I hoped it might be true when my subversive grandfather whispered to me that my mother and father weren't properly divorced. It doesn't seem so regrettable in retrospect, but his complaint was only that they'd got a civil divorce and not a rabbinical one.

Every time I visit Lexington and pass the house on Ashland Avenue where we waited out Shirley's honeymoon, I feel an urge to stop the car and ring the door-bell. I long to see over the house once again (for my memory of it is strong but imperfect) and to reassure myself that its current owners are keeping it in good repair. It has the appearance of an antebellum house, with widely spaced Greek Revival columns supporting a portico that extends the entire width of the front of the house, covering the wooden porch that encompasses the area beneath it. The house is faced in brick and the wooden surfaces are painted white. In fact I suspect it was built in the 1890s or even later.

Passionately though I loved that house, I can remember little about its geography, except for the living room with the radio and phonograph in their French-looking light wood console. I think the room was a double cube. It contained Lil's and Louis's usual furniture: the Louis XVI suite had been re-covered for the house in silk rep with wide ivory and vermillion stripes. The dining room may have been on the other side of the front hall from the living room, and I suppose one reached the kitchen from it. On the ground floor I only really remember the screened-in pantry-cum-larder at the back of the house, because it was there that one of the Jibbies ate the twenty-pound Thanksgiving turkey.

I was never allowed to have a dog of my own at Shirley's house, so it was understood that I had a small share in Lola's and Uncle Louis's dogs. These were always called Jibby, regardless of breed. The turkey-phage was a black cocker spaniel, by this time getting old. He was killed by a car in front of the house and I for a long time felt both grief and guilt, as I took the view that he had sacrificed himself for me. I had run across the road without looking properly; the half-blind Jibby had bounded along by my side, and the unseen oncoming car struck him instead of me. The fact that I wasn't chastised and that everyone seemed less concerned at Jibby's death than for my safety, made me feel worse.

It was a big house, and it rambled. There was a coach-house at the back, converted into a garage; it had a first floor which contained a flat or perhaps offices. I have a feeling I wasn't encouraged to explore there; maybe it was dilapidated and unsafe for prowling children. I do remember that, reached by a back staircase, was my room. I always had my own room, or a room shared with my brother, in each of Lola's houses. It contained a set of encyclopaedias, 'The Book of Knowledge', in an old-ish edition, which had probably belonged to Uncle Manuel Singer. I read a good deal of its volumes, almost unintentionally using the procedure of *sortes Vergilianae*: I simply picked any volume up at random and began reading where it fell open.

Life at Ashland Avenue seemed to be divided between my reading and listening to records (I learnt from 'Peter and the Wolf' to identify every instrument in the orchestra) and sitting on the floor in front of the radio for Jack Benny and Fibber McGee and Molly on Sunday nights, and Sky King, Batman and the Green Hornet (or was it the Green Lantern?) on schoolday afternoons.

Lola employed a pretty black maid, another Sally. We were fond of each other; I spent a lot of time in her company, and she would sometimes volunteer to look after me when she was off-duty. We had a long-standing date for her to take me to the circus. I can remember that we did indeed go to the circus, and that the sideshow of 'freaks' and two-headed sheep struck me as disgustingly sleazy. I have never been able to get the point of circus clowns; even then their tumbling and bumbling struck me as mere anarchy – not frightening or sinister, but without interest. Like any child I was thrilled by the animal acts and the trapeze artistes.

Of what followed, I remember very little concretely. We always joked about it as the episode when I was stolen by the Gypsies. I think what happened was that Sally offered to, as it were, take me backstage. In my mind's eye there is a campfire and a circle of people around it, with some caravans (neither modern 'mobile homes' nor old-fashioned painted wooden ones, though). Plump and yellow-haired, I was fussed over by a lot of swarthy people, some of whom were obviously of mixed blood, like Sally, who was caramel-coloured, and, I feel pretty certain, related to these Gypsies.

We got home much later than expected. Lil and Shirley were agitated but not frantic, as they knew we were going to the circus and were able to make allowance for our being an hour of two late. The remaining four or five hours Sally accounted for by saying, truthfully, that we had taken supper with some circus friends of hers, who, of course, had no access to the telephone. Her excuses were accepted, as it was unthinkable that she would allow any harm to come to me – and I had obviously had a thrilling day.

Did I relate my adventure at the next meeting of the Cub Scouts? Though it was just the sort of tale I relished telling and though it was certain to attract an admiring audience, I don't think we did that sort of thing in the Cubs, which basically consisted of some of the boys' mothers doing a good turn for the other mothers, by agreeing to be Den Mother, and feeding milk and cookies to a lot of unruly little boys once a week.

My more significant after-school activity was music. Lola is supposed to have played the violin. I don't think she was the reason I nagged my parents for violin lessons. I think Jascha Heifetz was my inspiration. Thus I began on a half-size fiddle hired from a downtown musical instruments shop. My teacher was called Miss Rubens, and I don't think it occurred to me (though it did to her) that me and my brother were the only Jews who had ever walked through the dismal doors of Picadome School. Miss Rubens was not local; in fact, I don't think she was even a southerner. She must have wandered into the Fayette County school system by mistake – perhaps she had come to Lexington to be with her man. She was very pretty and apparently single; there was a single Jewish man running the Youth Orchestra; maybe they were connected.

In any case I was very bad at playing the violin, and should have taken Miss Rubens's hint and changed to the 'cello or double bass where lapses of intonation were not so immediately obvious, and bowing technique so much easier. But I stubbornly and fruitlessly stuck to my fiddle. I began Saturday morning private lessons, first with her and then with a man (her boyfriend?), but to no avail. Really, I was hopeless. Not unmusical, but hopeless on the violin. My ear needed training, and the violin is not the instrument on which to improve a wobbly sense of intonation. (Singing is better, as I discovered much later.)

Children who played string instruments were grouped together in the 'orchestra', whereas those who elected brass, woodwind or percussion were in the 'band'. Obviously it was more macho to be in the band, where there was even the possibility of graduating into the uniformed marching band when we got to high school. But I did not even mind the cissy aspect of playing the violin in the orchestra. Wasn't I emulating Jascha in my own mind? And wasn't the orchestra culturally superior to the band. This was proved by the (albeit grudging) secondment of the best woodwind, brass and percussion players from the band to the orchestra.

Over the years, one thing remained constant. I got no better. Was I content to play second violin forever? I had a go at the 'cello, the double bass and, once, even a tuba or Sousaphone (on which I found it quite easy, at least, to produce a noise). But I soldiered (or rather, sawed) on, moving resiny fingers through the five positions, but never, so far as I can remember, making an attractive, let alone a beautiful sound.

After puberty, in Junior High School, I finally admitted to myself that I was ashamed of the essential effeminacy of playing the violin (while real boys played baseball), and contrived to lose the new fiddle my mother or father had only recently bought. I knew that if it just couldn't be found when school began in the autumn, there was no way anybody was going to replace it; I'd be admonished, but let off the hook. It was dead easy: I left it in the orchestra room when school broke up for the summer, in the certainty that someone would have stolen it by September, when school resumed.

We now lived, with Shirley and Babe, on Arcadia Park, a boring lower-middle-class neighbourhood, in which the houses were dull and so were the people. Except for fourteen- or fifteen-year-old May, who played the double bass and sometimes baby-sat for us; she was sexy, and I had hopes that she was going to indulge me in more than the occasional game of strip poker, the rules of which she taught me early on in our acquaintance. I regretted that she soon found a more suitable, older boy to satisfy her own randy urges. Apart from the Roman Catholic masturbation instructor, also a musician – a prodigy at the piano – and also too old to be a friend to an eight- or nine-year-old, there was nobody who interested me. I found our house unlikeable and my school a hell-hole. What a pity this was all mixed up in my head with my feelings about Shirley remarrying. Even Babe, with his sweet nature and infinite flexibility must have found me a pain.

My only amusing memory of the Arcadia Park house was that once, inspired by a comic-book version of Poe's 'Raven', I decided to become a poet. Naturally, I realised that writing verse was a nocturnal activity, so in my dressing gown and slippers, I erected a makeshift verse-composing desk at the top of the first-floor landing. I was hard at work on an epic whose subject was, I think, an up-coming college football match (which held no interest at all for me *per se*, but I think I realised that classic poetry mustn't be subjective). Babe and Shirley were out, and May was, no doubt, snogging with her boyfriend in the living room. She would, in any case, not have heard anything till my brother hit the bottom of the staircase. He was walking in his sleep (I knew all about somnambulism from my comic book Edgar Allen Poe) and would certainly have taken a tumble down the stairs had I not been dallying with Calliope at the top.

Comic books were my chief mode of learning. Every Sunday we spent with Murph, usually at his parents's house. It was not on the whole, a treat. He seemed to sense this, and after the not usually very digestible lunch provided by his mother (the chicken soup always had a few tiny globules of golden fat floating on its surface, a gastronomic turn-off, I found), he took us downtown to the Fayette Cigar Store where we were allowed to choose ten comics each. They cost ten cents each, so we each had a dollar's spending-power a week.

The effect this had on our popularity in the neighbourhood would be hard to exaggerate. Between us we had twenty *new* comics a week; this meant that there was no hero with whose deeds we could not keep abreast. Superman, Wonder Woman, Batman, Captain Marvel – we had complete files of their adventures. Our budget would even stretch to new characters such as Plastic Man, horror comics, such as 'Tales from the Crypt', when they were invented halfway through my childhood, and blatant rip-offs, such as Superboy and Wonder Girl, that made fools like us part with our parents' money to read spurious stories about the infancy and childhood of our heroes. For the rest of the kids in Arcadia Park, our house was a lending library of all that was newest, best and most desirable in contemporary fiction.

My tastes soon changed, and I left the neighbourhood kids behind – at some cost to my social standing. I got hooked on 'Classics Illustrated', coloured strip-cartoon versions of real books, with whole passages from the originals intact. From them you could, for example, not only learn the plot of, say,

Macbeth, but 'Tomorrow and tomorrow and tomorrow creeps in this petty pace . . .' Oh, well, I was a bookish child, and in this painless way I absorbed great chunks of English literature (Dickens, the Brontës, Scott), American (Melville, Hawthorne, Poe) and even French (Victor Hugo and both Dumas). To this day I have strong visual impressions of characters in the standard works of literature.

It never occurred to me that this was either a cheap way to become lettered, or that it was cheating. In fact, it predisposed me to learn vast tracts of verse by heart. And it left me free to read what I really wanted – Mickey Spillaine. Did Shirley and Babe really allow me to help myself to the latest Mike Hammer as soon as they'd finished it? Could they have realised that Shirley's nine-year-old was reading *New York Confidential* only a week after they themselves had finished these mildly pornographic paperbacks? In my double bed, with the door to my room locked, I ploughed through the best-seller list of junk fiction. It did me no harm at all, as I was catholic, and read Raymond Chandler, whose style counteracted the gush of *Gone with the Wind* and *Forever Amber*.

Before I was a voracious reader, I was a voracious listener. The one thing I remember about Murph was his reading to me when I was very small indeed. I not only had the usual nursery books – of which I remember *Struwwelpeter* with fascinated distaste – but several *Wizard of Oz* books, and, most especially, Murph read most or all of *Idylls of the King*. My childish head was not only filled with King Arthur, Sir Lancelot, Merlin and Guinevere, but with ideas of poetic diction: all knights 'from the proud tower came'.

When I was a little older, Murph, the Rooseveltian liberal made certain that the books in the nursery instilled right thinking. I remember two anti-racist titles in particular. One was called *Nicodemus and Santa Claus*. The plot dealt with the unkindness and misbehaviour of a little white boy to a little black one. Christmas came, and the little white boy had an empty stocking. Nicodemus, the long-suffering black boy, on the other hand, was inundated with goodies. On the last page of this illustrated book it was revealed that Father Christmas was a black man.

Even more to my literary taste, in a way, was *Churkendoose*, a tale of everyday farmyard miscegenation. The book was accompanied by a record narrated and sung by Ray Bolger, the tin man of *The Wizard of Oz*, who lamented at one point, 'I'd rather be a chicken or a turkey or a duck or a goose./ But I can't be one of them: I'm a churkendoose.' In the end, the ugly poultry specimen turns out to have hybrid vigour, and rescues all the farm creatures from the attentions of the fox. I got the message and grew quite sentimental over it, though, even as a child, I think I recognised it as kitsch.

From Sunday lunchtime on we were Murph's. But Shirley had succeeded in making Sunday mornings painful to him. Following the divorce, she refused to let us go any longer to Sunday school at the synagogue. She struck a serious blow against Orthodoxy, by insisting that, if we were to have any religious education at all, it was to be at the more liberal Reform Temple. Murph hated this, as he considered Reform Judaism to be a sect of Protestant Christianity. No keeping kosher, and organ music during services. Besides, the temple was the preserve of the German Jews (who had, of course, done the original Reforming of the Jewish religion) who were all snobs. Never mind that most of Murph's Jewish friends were German Jews, to the extent that Barbara Hymson (who was a bit older than me) once explained to me that her *Litvak* family and my own were 'honorary German Jews' for social purposes.

Nonetheless, Murph did not like collecting us at noon from the Temple, to drive us to see if Mr Goller had any bagels left before going home to his mother for lunch. She, of course, was thunderstruck by our enforced defection from the synagogue (which, actually, delighted us). To her, we might as well have gone to Church and received Holy Communion, thus desecrating our mouths for the sacrament of her chicken soup.

Sunday school was a scream. The first teacher I can remember was Dr Hahn, a kindly old German psychology professor at Transylvania, who treated our class as a ready-made if not quite random sample for his own research. Each Sunday brought forth a new test. We had IQ tests, reading ability tests, ink blot tests, spatial configuration tests, and, most fun of all, memory tests that involved seeing how many digits of a number you could recite back to Dr Hahn after hearing them only once, or for the adept (of which I was one), recite backwards.

There was no God-bothering in Dr Hahn's class, and no nonsense about Bible stories either. This pagan Golden Age could not last forever, and soon the ten or twelve of us in our class (war babies, we were the largest group of kids in the Sunday school for many years) were consigned to the care of the schoolteacher, lawyer or psychiatrist who had volunteered to give up his or her Sunday morning – in exchange for the right to exercise a little power over other people's children.

We recognised that this should be so, and didn't object too much. What we minded was religion. It wasn't a question of theology; as nine- and ten-year-olds we didn't care much whether God existed. Why then, were we militantly irreligious? Partly we were reacting to the patent hypocrisy of our non-believing or at best lukewarm parents; and partly we were cross with them, I suppose, for insisting that we inconvenience ourselves on Sunday morning to learn about something that set us apart from our everyday schoolmates.

Most of all though, I think we sensed that our parents were unconsciously trying to create psychological ghetto conditions for their children, by forcing us to socialise with other Jewish children. (I was snobbishly thankful that my mother had intervened to the extent of allowing me to serve my time with the presentable children of the Temple rather than the less couth lot at the synagogue.) They were protecting us from the gentile world that banned them from their country clubs, and that spurned their mostly Yankee accents (my father was exceptional in having been born in Lexington; most of my friends' parents were emigrés from the north or east). Their children, born to drawl, would have preferred to take their chances in the world as they found it.

We were thus rebellious from an early age. Our best prank was done early on in my Sunday school career. Norma Wikler, Judy Goldfarb and I so exasperated our teacher one Sunday – probably by refusing to shut up and listen to the history of Moses' discovery in the bullrushes, or something similar – that he told us to leave. We agreed that, though he had slung us out, he hadn't told us to stay in the building. It was early spring and the first shrubs were in flower. So we decided to perform a miracle.

With my penknife we cut many, many sprays of forsythia, each of the three of us splaying out the spindly branches until we had enough to represent a small bush. We then promenaded under the high windows of the classroom from which we'd been expelled; we could not be seen from inside, but the ambulatory forsythia shrubs could. We marched back and forth silently, until the miracle of the moving forsythia bushes caused a proper commotion inside the building. We cut and ran to a position from which we could observe but not be observed, and watched as our confederates argued, as we knew we could count on them to do, that there was no essential difference between what they had just witnessed and the episode of Moses and the burning bush. A harassed and impotent teacher now had to deal not only with insubordination, but with blasphemy.

Years later this same teacher had a nervous breakdown that sent him to hospital; if I remember rightly, he blamed my brother for his condition. This should not be taken lightly. When my brother was eight, he was given a ventriloquist's dummy. Edgar Bergen and his dummy, Charlie McCarthy, were all the rage on the radio, and it was hoped that my brother's undoubted talent for speaking without moving his lips would make him popular with the other children, who might then not notice that my brother was scarcely bigger than his dummy. He applied this skill to driving his primary school teacher, Mrs Symonds, mad. He was helped in this project by a surrealist sense of humour. One day Mrs Symonds was giving a slide projector tour of world monuments. When she came to the famous statue of Napoleon at Les Invalides she asked, 'Now, children, why is Napoleon always depicted with his hand inside his jacket?' 'Please, Miz Symonds,' piped up my brother, 'that's where he keeps his cheese sandwich'. Lola was summoned to the school (they couldn't reach Shirley) and asked to remove Sandy. She was in time to see Mrs Symonds carted away in the ambulance by the men in white coats.

I must not give the impression that I had escaped altogether from the synagogue. There was still the matter of the bar mitzvah, the ceremony of tribal manhood, when the Jewish boy reaches thirteen, and becomes eligible to be called upon to read the law, the sacred scroll of the Torah, in the synagogue, and when his presence counts to make up the quorum of ten required to hold a religious service. The Temple had abolished this rite or had never celebrated it. (Reform Jews, Protestant to the point of being Anglicans, had substituted Confirmation for both boys and girls for the pointedly sexist bar mitzvah.) My father's mother would have perished for shame if I had not been bar mitzvah; even Shirley could see that. So from the age of ten or eleven I was packed off once a week after school to 'Hebrew school', to prepare for my thirteenth birthday.

Never was anything so mis-called as 'Hebrew school'. In the first place it had only three pupils, Dick Munich, Mike Ades and me, in order of descending age. In the second place, it seldom had a teacher, and nothing was actually taught. We were drilled by rote by a still older boy, Casey Newman (another nephew of my uncle Louis), who taught us the liturgy. (Could he carry a tune? I don't remember; and it didn't much matter, as the congregation was accustomed to chanting any old series of notes that came into their heads.)

A rabbi was finally found to teach us, just in time for my bar mitzvah; but that, too, made no difference. He had no more idea of teaching us Hebrew as a language than did young Casey. My head is still full of snatches of tunes in minor keys with words I remember but don't understand: that is the sole legacy of my afternoons spent at the synagogue. It was difficult to get there, too. One had to take a combination of buses from school and walk quite a distance; I have blotted out the whole painful memory, except that the afternoon sometimes ended with a game of football or basketball at Dick Munich's house. The other two boys soon learnt that I was hopeless at anything involving a ball, and allowed me to retire with some grace to the sidelines.

Though my grandmother died when I was still twelve, I was not let off the bar mitzvah. It now had to be gone through with 'for the sake of her memory'. So in late February, 1954, witnessed by, among others, my seventh grade teacher and my music teacher, who claimed to be flattered to have been asked, I mounted the pulpit and sang a portion of the Torah, whose words and melody I had committed to memory. I don't think I made any mistakes, but the experience was extremely painful.

I mean that literally. I had poison ivy on my balls. While the new rabbi was wittering on about the moral lessons to be learnt from my stamp collection and today-he-is-a-man, I was learning a theology lesson: God existed, He performed miracles and He was malevolent. Poison ivy, *Rhus radicans*, only exists in North America; I suffered so badly from the contact rash it inflicts upon those sensitive to it, that it gave me sufficient reason to emigrate. Even so, the noxious weed doesn't grow in Kentucky in the winter and, in any case, I was not out and about exposing my scrotum in the woods where it grows.

Our family doctor, Franklin Moosnick, who was confident of his diagnosis of poison ivy rash, but bewildered by its genesis, said he thought the toxic element in the plant could be airborne in smoke if anyone burned it. But who could burn it in February? So in front of the sacred scroll, I tugged, scratched and mentally cursed the God who had chosen to demonstrate He was Boss by performing this uncomfortable miracle.

I got even. I never went to the synagogue again.

Chapter Seven

One question I am asked by anyone who hears me speak and who knows anything about my background: what happened to my American accent? When I explain that my natal dialect was southern, it always seems to lessen the urgency of the question. Nobody – especially no American – expects anybody to keep a southern accent. To do so would not only be eccentric, but hard work. Very few of my Lexington friends retain the speech of childhood; an exception is Elizabeth Hardwick, who is of a generation senior to mine – and I think she has gone to more trouble to keep her attractive drawl than I ever did to discard my own.

What does it sound like, this celebrated dialect? On the radio in my childhood, it was thought to be funny if spoken by a Negro, like Jack Benny's Rochester, but indicative of a lack of education when emanating from the mouth of a white character. We who spoke it in real life tended to share the stereotype, though we allowed room for the further one of the southern belle, who, so long as she was pretty, well brought up and, better still, rich, could say 'y'all' till the cows came home without a word of reproach from anyone.

There were degrees of drawling: the speech of the natives got slower, thicker and contained more syllables per word the further south you went. I never heard any human language less intelligible than that spoken in Biloxi, Mississippi and parts of southern Louisiana until I once got stranded in central

Yugoslavia. We Lexington-speakers were relatively civilised, and could be understood readily by any unprejudiced listener. I was not self-conscious about my accent and did not set out to lose it. What happened was that my parents sent us each summer for three years, which for me was between the ages of nine and eleven, to a summer camp on the shores of Lake Erie, conveniently close for the Cleveland relatives to keep an eye on us. Four or five boys from Lexington – all Jewish and, of necessity well-heeled – went to Camp Roosevelt, and all of us lost our drawls as soon as possible after our first week's experience of this no longer predominantly WASP institution (by the time we went it was about half Jewish). The reason was simple: we were the only boys from the south, and we were persecuted mightily until we conformed to the prevalent mid-western twang, a linguistic amalgam of Cleveland, Buffalo and up-state New York and Pittsburgh.

It was unlovely to hear, but did sound more sophisticated than our own speech. We were teased, even punished, until we could do a passable imitation of its clipped vowels and articulated 'r's. (There is no terminal 'r' in the Lexington dialect; indeed, 'r' is only pronounced at the beginning of a word and after a consonant, and is normally silent after a vowel.) I soon learnt to switch off my drawl as soon as I stepped off the Pullman train at Cleveland. That was all right; the only problem was switching it back on again. It took a good month of being back at school before I could sound anything like the Picadome yokels. None of the Lexington Roosevelt camper-victims ever drawled again. Most of them were only made to spend one summer in this expensive bondage, and managed to convince their parents that it would be cruel to send them back to serve another sentence. I grew to like it.

To imagine life at Camp Roosevelt (campers were known collectively as Rough Riders – the Roosevelt in question was Teddy) you have to think of an entire year at an English public school compressed into eight weeks, a wrong-way telescope-image of boarding school existence. As the fees for the two months were greater than those for a year at Eton, you can understand how the owners could afford to leave their plant idle for the remaining ten months. (It must have been very profitable; the fees were, I think $2000, and, as it was the convention to employ mainly trainee 'counsellors', the wages bill could not have been large.)

The entire camp, from the youngest six-year-old bed-wetters' brigade, which included my unhappy brother, to the pubescent fifteen-year-olds, were organised into two tribes, given the Indian names 'Sioux' and 'Chips' (presumably short for Chippewas). The counsellors were called 'Blackfeet'. We were pitted against each other in deadly competition, and got points for such things as our prowess at shooting, archery, riding, military drill, swimming, rowing, baseball, tennis and even for having the tidiest cabin. Our uninsulated, wooden cabins, each with a dozen or so bunks, were inspected at least weekly. The owners saved even more in wages because we were made to do our own domestic chores (except for our laundry). It was there I learnt to make a bed with hospital corners so tight that you can bounce a coin off it.

I also learnt to shoot a rifle with some accuracy, to paddle a canoe and to tell lies. Not just ordinary lies, mind you, but Scheherezade-style whoppers, and basically for the same reason – to entertain. Perhaps I was just serving an apprentice-ship at constructing a narrative. Most of my tales were shaggy-horse stories, rambling, plotless anecdotes about life among the Thoroughbreds of Lexington, in which I won countless awards for equestrian feats in glamorous local horse shows. I had a receptive audience.

Though I was always last to be chosen for the side in any sport, and even humbled by being relegated to right field when playing softball, I astonished my real best friend Mitch, a born athlete himself, by being put in the group with the best riders. I say 'real' best friend, because Mitch was another Lexington boy, and we've kept up our friendship as grown men. But Camp Roosevelt resembled an English public school in another respect: there was an underground current of romantic friendships among some of the boys. Mostly, and in my own case, this was sublimated; but I did once walk into a cabin – not my own – one day when it could have been expected to be empty, and saw two boys my own age, both athletes, doing surprising things to each other. Group masturbation was commonplace: there was even a rape variation, in which four or five boys would pin one boy to his bed and wank him. Homosexual behaviour with a sentimental component was, however, rare. We left that to the counsellors, who as near as one could tell, came in only two varieties: those who made pregnant the female counsellors at Wingfoot, the sister girls' camp fifteen miles away, and those who had taken the job because they liked the company of boys younger than themselves.

My Arabian Nights tales were not constructed for Mitch, who in any case would have known them to be false, but for a boy, smaller, blonder and a better rider than myself, on whom I had a crush. Willie had an entourage: he attracted a circle of boys our own age, and it was for them – but especially for him – that I spun my yarns. There were real pleasures to be had from Camp Roosevelt: long overnight trips by canoe or on horseback, further along Lake Erie, which had not then been poisoned, and whose waters were sweet and inhabited by fish. Whether they were worth a year's school fees, I leave to someone else's judgement. The main purpose of sending your children to a summer camp was, after all, to get them out of your hair for two months, and in that it succeeded completely.

Something happened in my last year at Roosevelt that helped me to grow up a good deal. I behaved badly to someone and felt real shame about it. The counsellor in our cabin, whom I'll call Ron, was a boy of nineteen or twenty from somewhere like Pittsburgh. I think he was Jewish, but he was not from the same privileged background as the campers. Perhaps he was working his way through college, and this was his summer job. He was introspective and, to tell the truth, creepy. The chip on his shoulder was heavy, and as uncomfortable for us as for him. We eleven-year-old campers were unresponsive to his surly requests and his black moods. At first we showed our disapproval in the normal ways: we made him an apple-pie bed ('short-sheeted' in local parlance, for the bottom sheet was folded upwards at only two-thirds of its length, in the hope that the victim would get into his bed too vigorously and rip the sheet), placed a bucket of water on a short length of wood over the door of the cabin – just as we saw him coming to enter it, and made him the subject of a whispering campaign. A more mature, more secure man would have treated this as a form of hazing, and seen it as the affectionate teasing veterans hand out to novices.

But not Ron; he bit his nails closer to the quick and made himself even less agreeable to his charges. We were on the point of mutiny: we'd swept the cabin, dusted it, and removed the cobwebs for the umpteenth time, and just were not going to do it again. (Ron was neurotic about the week-end inspection, feeling that our lack of house-pride was a reflection on him.)

I, of course, was the ring-leader. We were quite prepared to ask for him to be transferred to another cabin. But first I spoke to him, and said that if he would only listen to our wishes sometimes, and try to smile a little, we would co-operate with him. He confessed his own unhappiness, and further confided in me that he was a bit of a fish out of water. I gave him sympathy, and an assurance that we'd all have a go at getting on.

A few moments later, I was standing in front of a hedge dividing one part of the camp from another, when my friend Bob Miller, an older Lexington boy who was then a counsellor, and had been taking an interest in the Ron saga, asked me how our talk had gone. 'I've got him,' I boasted, 'eating out of my hand.' A rustle in the shrubbery revealed the lurking presence of the betrayed Ron. Though I choked on my shame, there was no way I could take my Judas-words back. Ron asked to go to another cabin, and he was replaced in ours by handsome, feckless Hank, who let us go our own way while he concentrated on getting one of the Wingfoot girls pregnant.

In retrospect, my last summer at camp was less inglorious than the two preceding ones had been. I was getting better at sport – even progressing from right field to catcher in the softball team – and gaining in poise even when not on the back of a horse. One reason for this was the onset of puberty, so early that it gave me kudos amongst the envious eleven boys who saw me dress and undress daily.

That summer my voice broke. As though she had never dealt with a pubescent boy, the silly camp nurse decided that my croaks meant something sinister and confined me to the infirmary until the time came around for the camp doctor's weekly visit. Mitch's parents Irv (a psychiatrist) and Ada (she of the pickles) turned up that year on visitors' day (it was a 'fur piece' to come from Lexington) and Ada said, 'Why, your voice is changing,' disposing of my 'symptoms' in a sentence.

There was another reason. For my first two years at camp, I had been known, universally and humiliatingly, as 'Fats'. I remember well the first day of this last year, when, viewing the new, svelte me, one of the boys had said they could no longer call me by that hurtful (but formerly truthful) nickname.

At eleven, I was still in the care of the town's paediatrician, Dr Maxwell. At the beginning of the year, he had decided that my tummy was worse than unsightly. I suppose, noticing the signs of puberty, he had decided that he was no longer dealing with puppy fat. So he used what may perhaps have been the only remedy available to him in 1952, and put me on dexedrine. I was re-born, newly minted, full of energy, a natural leader of boys, if not of men. No wonder: I was on speed for a whole year.

Unsurprisingly, the pounds melted away and, as I shot up to nearly my full height before I reached thirteen, I was remarkably sightly and even well-proportioned. I wish somebody had told me this, though. While I certainly enjoyed the improvements in my figure and fortunes, I was still mentally a fat boy, always just a few pounds overweight in my mind. I needed retraining at reading my image in the mirror. By the time Dr Kavka had got me on the couch, it was too late for me to change my picture of myself as fundamentally chubby. Too bad, for not only would I have enjoyed my adolescence more, but I might not have given up the struggle so easily when I started putting weight back on in my mid-twenties. (I have learnt, sadly, that the process of putting weight back on is never finished; eventually you learn to live comfortably in your own ever-expanding clothes.)

The improvement in my fortunes I owed to the fact that we had moved. Babe and Shirley had bought a house on Indian Mound Road, named because it had, presumably, been the site of Indian burial mounds. I dug up half our back garden, but failed to confirm the archaeological value of our new property. Still, we were back on the right side of the tracks. This even meant a new school for me, nice, safely middleclass Kenwick, albeit for only one year, as I was in the sixth and final grade of elementary school.

This was my *annus mirabilis*. I was at a new school, one where good manners were encouraged (what a little prig I was), and the yokel element, not at all rough, was represented only by a sprinkling of quite nice people with benign Mountain accents. There was one country boy, a member of the huge Ritchie family from eastern Kentucky, who was backward. He had failed the sixth grade so often that he was practically a grown man, and towered above us. He was amiable, couldn't read, and didn't seem to mind being kept behind with the children while his peers went on to high school or jobs.

One day the debauched member of a pair of twins (the other of whom was as sanctimonious as his brother was wicked) let his curiosity get the better of him, and interfered with the (perfectly compliant) giant in the boys loo. Somehow the female teacher found out about it, marched in and broke it up. There was hell to pay for the malefactor. At least he didn't suffer the fate of poor Lulu, a dim girl who'd also been at my first school. Lulu got pregnant and had a baby while we were still in the sixth grade, which should have been a terrible warning to us all, but somehow struck us as too ludicrous to allow the drawing a moral.

Although I was a new boy that autumn, I soon made my mark. Against the advice of our teacher, who was very sympathetic to me, but said that I couldn't be expected to do very well in a school-wide election, my class nominated me for election as a 'patrol boy', and I won. My mother was dismayed. She knew very well that this was the highest honour available at the school, that it meant that I was popular and well settled in my new school. But it also meant that I had to be at school half an hour before it started, to help the younger children cross the road and to keep order, and so couldn't travel to school by the school bus. Wearily and reluctantly, she agreed to drive me the five or six miles to school each morning. I had no trouble getting up early: thanks to Dr Maxwell, I was still speeding.

The spring of the following year my parents allowed me to go on a supervised trip to New Orleans. It was not exactly a school trip, for the children who went were drawn from all the schools of the town, including 'U. High', the private school attached to the University of Kentucky. This meant that both my friend Mitch and my older friend Barbara Hymson went too. The trip may have been supervised, but once we got off the train our chaperones were not much in evidence. I could scarcely decide what hell to raise first.

I chose to begin my life of adult vice by drinking a lot of coffee. Coffee was forbidden to children at home because, back in Cleveland, Shirley had known a little boy whose parents allowed him to drink coffee from his infancy. He died at a very young age (probably, my brother and I speculated, run over by a trailer truck). New Orleans coffee was mixed with chicory. I had never tasted coffee before, and I was pleased to see that if you put enough cream and sugar in it, it actually tasted good. Next I bought two packets of cigarettes, and smoked all forty of them, one after another, in the bedroom I shared with a very amused Mitch, who watched with dispassionate humour.

Then I went out to dinner with Hymson (I always called her that, never Barbara) at Arnaud's – we couldn't get a table at the better-known Antoine's – with some of the older kids. I ordered a bottle of wine. The waiter brought it, poured some in my glass, and I tasted it. Just then one of our scarce chaperones made an appearance and, as ill luck would have it, she was one who knew I was only thirteen years old. She confiscated the bottle, which was more humiliating for the older, but still under-age kids, than for me, who had proved myself both daring and sophisticated.

Now, made confident by the waiter's lax acceptance of me as being old enough to drink, I was ready for real dissipation. The next afternoon, I ambled along to Bourbon Street, walked boldly into a jazz club, sat at the bar, and waited for a B-girl to join me. It took less than a minute. I knew exactly what to expect. Had I not read Babe's and Shirley's copy of *New Orleans Confidential*? I ordered Bourbon on the rocks; so did she. It was brought; I paid the bartender a fortune and gave him 25 cents tip as well. I choked down my Bourbon; she sipped what I knew from *New Orleans Confidential* was really iced tea. I forget what we talked about; it didn't really matter, as I knew from my book that she wasn't actually a prostitute, and that she made her living by being paid by the house to drink with the clients. I made my excuses and left, reeling from the effects of the first drink I had ever had away from the cushioning bosom of my family, and scurried back to the hotel to boast to Hymson and to Mitch, who didn't believe me.

I had been drunk once, a few weeks earlier. I cannot think what possessed Shirley (perhaps it was pride in her brand new house), but she proposed to hold a Passover seder for the Meyers family and her own. This did not get me off the hook of going to Murph's family, but they celebrated the seder for two nights, and could spare me for one. Our seder was a wonderful shambles. Uncle Manuel Meyers, as the oldest, was made to conduct the dinner. He hadn't a clue, and I don't think he could read Hebrew, so we read a few perfunctory words of English, and abandoned the formal part of the proceedings as soon as we had got through the mandatory four glasses of wine.

Shirley had not been to a seder for years; she had forgotten (or wished to ignore) the fact that Passover wineglasses are usually thimble-sized. She set the table (or Rhoda did) with full-sized five or six ounce glasses, and it was four of those every man, woman and child drank. Anyway, I did. The talk turned rude, raucous, obscene and very funny. I don't remember who suggested it, but the table was cleared and removed, and before long we were down on our knees shooting craps. Tootsie gave me a tutorial, explaining all about your 'point', 'snake-eyes', scores of seven or eleven, and 'crapping out'. Soon I was nudging Uncle Manuel to give me my turn. I lost. He took my money, saying in his W. C. Fields voice, 'Goddamn kid's gotta learn the hard way.'

My father's family would not have approved. But they didn't know. I felt no guilt – not even through my first hangover.

For about one year I was a Boy Scout. My scouting career was short, because the troop, though it was not all Jewish, met inconveniently at the Temple, and because I was not good material. The lowest rank was, I think, called Tenderfoot, and Tenderfoot I remained, though I was able to acquire the odd merit badge for lanyard-making and leaf-collecting. From my scouting days I retain nothing but an abiding suspicion of the motives of men who volunteer to be scoutmasters and strong convictions about the sexual predilections of the boys who remain scouts long enough to attain the senior ranks. These prejudices are based on my experience that summer of scout camp when, in our crowded six-person tent, an Eagle scout unzipped and climbed by turns into the sleeping bag of every scout junior to him in the hierarchy.

To compensate us for not going back to Camp Roosevelt this summer, Murph devised an elaborate holiday. He engaged a young man, a family friend called Alan, to share the driving with him, and we set off for Canada. Armed with several volumes of science fiction and half-a-lifetime's supply of 'Classics Illustrated' comics, I enjoyed the entire ambitious adventure. Sandy, generally car-sick in the back seat, pined for the lesser miseries of Camp Roosevelt, where he had only had to put up with bullying and his own bed-wetting.

We drove through Buffalo, where I was not surprised to learn we had relatives, and saw Niagara Falls first from the American, then from the Canadian side. As soon as we'd got to the latter, we learnt that we must not say 'American' when we meant 'US', as Canadians also consider themselves Americans. This presented some difficulties in adjective-formation, and we decided to leave the Canadians to sort out their own problems: we would go on calling ourselves Americans. Niagara Falls was reasonably awesome, but we had seen it in too many movies to be surprised by it. I have in my mind a picture of it being turned off, as though someone has turned a stopcock and shut off the water supply, leaving only rocky shelves and escarpments. Was this true? Is it a fantasy? Or is it something I only read about that happened many years later, when advances in technology allowed the flow of water to be stopped so repairs could be made to the eroded rock?

English-speaking Canada held little interest for me, and except for endless nights in 'motor hotels' – 'motel' was a neologism more often found on the other side of the border – I remember nothing until we reached Montreal and Quebec. We stayed for a bit at an old grand hotel – was it called Château Frontenac? – and I tried unsuccessfully to climb the hundreds of steps of the shrine of Sainte Ann de Beaupré on my knees along with the pilgrims and cure-seekers who left their sticks and crutches at the top as proofs of the many miracles effected there by the BVM. Apart from the *patates frites* the food, unusually, made no impression on me.

We tootled back slowly, through New England, stopping at Yale, Harvard and Princeton. In Cambridge, Massachusetts, after touring Harvard, Murph asked me how I had liked Yale. 'Not much,' I replied. 'Good', said Murph, standing on the steps of Widener Library, 'because you're going to college here.' In the library itself, in too loud a voice, Murph pointed out to me a black student, hunched over his books, so smartly dressed that he was the personification of Ivy League values and style. 'See him,' Murph stage-whispered. 'He belongs here. He's got here by his own merits, and he's just as good as the white boys who are studying with him. That's a lesson you must never forget.' Eyes welling with the tears of southern guilt, I, who had no racial feelings at all, promised my father that I had learnt all about racial equality this day. (When, years later, I was an undergraduate at the University of Chicago, and spent more time picketing for racial equality in front of Woolworths than I did in the classroom, I answered Murph's complaints by reminding him of the lesson he taught me at Harvard. He was unmoved.)

We had one more lesson in racial equality, I'm afraid. At a resort hotel in the New York Finger Lakes, we were turned away after Murph had signed the hotel register. The clerk apologetically explained that the hotel was 'restricted', but said there was another a few miles away that would welcome the four of us. I was puzzled. Murph explained that this meant that Jews were not allowed, and that though nobody would think us Jewish except for our name, he was certainly not going to play the game by the anti-Semites' rules.

The best thing about this entire long vacation was that Murph was tolerant of children's needs to be entertained, and we stopped at every amusement park on our route in this pre-Disney world. I revelled in Old Orange, Maine: the entire town seemed to be one big fun fair. Is it still there?

Not only Babe and Shirley had moved house; so had Lola and Uncle Louis, and they'd really done it in style this time. Curiously enough, they had only moved one house along, from a biggish modern house on Chinoe (pronounced shin'-o-ee) Road to what looked like the biggest house in town, on the corner of Chinoe and Richmond Road. The new house, faced in local stone, was situated in isolation on top of at least an acre of lawn that sloped down to the Richmond Road, and made the rich men's mansions in the two or three blocks to its left look modest. Access to the front door was by a path on the side of the house which was reached from the circular drive situated at the back of the house. It was intimidating, but some brave travellers would make their way to the front door and ask if it was a motel. They were invariably embarrassed to learn it was a private house.

The mistake was a reasonable one. Lola and Uncle Louis moved into the house in 1952. It had been built recently and was a bungalow, what was locally called a 'ranch-house', meaning no more than that it was a single-storey dwelling. This house simply sprawled over its huge plot of land: it took two or three minutes to walk from the bedroom wing that housed Lola's and Uncle Louis's bedroom, as well as separate rooms for Sandy and me, plus another guest bedroom, through a higher-ceilinged drawing room, from which you turned right for the front hall, or left for another reception room that held the drinks tray and an elegant Chinese red lacquer card table and chairs, through kitchen, pantry and laundry – which contained a full-sized mangle – on one side, or, on the other, through a large formal dining room, which led into the office, with two desks, a wall safe and the shelves that housed the mechanical bank collection, to the other end of the house, containing Tootsie's bedroom and bathroom. That had formerly been the maid's quarters and had an outside entrance. The back garden had a shuffleboard court painted on to a stretch of the drive, and a large kennels.

These they bought with their inhabitants, a pair of very young springer spaniel puppies. Circumstances caught us out here, as we had only one name for dogs; so the one who was not Jibby became Jibby's Brother. Brother was officially assigned to my ownership, though he continued to reside at the Richmond Road house. That didn't matter, because I practically lived there too. We had a small tragedy, however. Brother, though not Jibby, fell ill. Distemper was diagnosed, and the vet said he would have to be 'put to sleep' the next day. Lola wisely let me stay up all night cuddling my puppy, so that I was exhausted, but prepared to part with him when morning came. I'd never known anything could be so sad.

There were cheerful times too, as when I was allowed to bring the whole of my class from Kenwick School to watch the Coronation on the new, rare television set that stood proudly in the drawing room. Everyone was suitably impressed with my standard of living, even if it wasn't my parents' house.

It was at Richmond Road that I remember food beginning to be interesting. Lola was not a bad cook herself, but she was seldom in the kitchen. She taught her repertory of dishes to her various cooks. It wasn't large, and the dish I remember best was called 'chicken fricassee'. Made with tiny spicy meatballs as well as chicken, and served in tomato-based sauce, it had absolutely nothing to do with the genuine French creamy *fricassée*, and was, I am told by a friend who is doing research into American Jewish food, strictly a Jewish recipe of Eastern European origin. I had always imagined it was southern.

Tootsie occasionally took a turn in the kitchen and produced dishes with Yiddish names, such as *Gedempte Fleisch*, braised brisket of beef, or *Blintzes*, blini stuffed with a curd cheese filling. The crêpes, which I think she called *Bletlach*, were eggier than normal ones. *Blintzes* were normally eaten with home-made jam, and the contrast of the sweetness with the slight acid of the cheese filling was very good. Tootsie was not a great cook, and her *Knaidlach* or matzoh balls and *Kreplach*, meat-filled ravioli shaped accompaniments to chicken soup, were no better than my other grandmother's.

Any Jew reading this is probably quivering with indignation at this worst of all insults to a grandmother's memory, so let me be quick to add that Tootsie made exquisite *Mandelbröt*, those hard, crunchy almond biscuits first formed into a flat loaf and then sliced, that figure in the cuisines of many lands. I once had a remarkably similar sweet biscuit in China. We were, I think, in a culinary blind alley: a non-kosher household with nothing but kosher recipes. We were definitely not consuming the fat of the land, except at the Christmas country ham and egg nog binge.

Babe's Indian dishes provided relief at home. At Richmond Road, culinary deliverance came from a series of black maids. The first I remember clearly was called Mattie. She was more than half white and had come, I should think, from Louisiana, as her cooking was French-inspired Creole. (It must have been Mattie who had worked briefly for Eleanor Roosevelt and could not get used to Lil hanging up her own clothes: 'Miz Roosevelt jes' lef' hu-uh clothes on de floor whe'h she took 'em off, an' Ah hung 'em up in de mawnin'.') How Mattie could cook.

Chicken now came, not only fried, but braised in a thickened red wine sauce with squares of fat-back bacon, mushrooms and baby onions. Or it turned up with rice in jambalaya. I encountered okra for the first time, in gumbo. And at Thanksgiving or Christmas, scalloped oysters (bought 'shucked' in their liquor) in a creamy sauce topped with a layer of crushed cream crackers. Strawberry shortcake, in its season, was a dessert with which we were already familiar; to this, Mattie added charlotte, the mould lined with liquor-soaked sponge fingers, and filled with pulped strawberries and cream, and a coffee-flavoured gelatine-stiffened pudding I would later come to know as a *bavarois*. Mattie usually served us at table. An electric buzzer, hidden under the carpet, replaced the green rooster-bell. Lil would buzz; Mattie would always seem to know what the signal meant and would issue from the kitchen, either with second helpings or with a tray to clear away the empty plates.

Mattie left, but her replacement was an even better cook. The only difficulty was a purely nominal one, for the new cook bore Lola's forename attached to Shirley's married name. She was Lillian Myers. The problem was solved by always referring to her as 'Lillian'. Lillian was enormous, so large in girth that she had to go through most doors sideways. She tired easily too, and cooked sitting on a high stool. She liked using the mangle to iron the sheets, because that had to be done sitting down in order to operate the controls.

Lillian's greatest dish was chocolate pudding. Lillian's chocolate pudding was a mousse made from nothing but Baker's unsweetened chocolate, sugar and egg yolks, usually garnished with nothing but sugarless thick whipped cream. She would serve this in a large glass gratin dish that fitted into a special heavy silver tray. The only lily-gilding allowed was the infrequent addition of rum- or brandy-soaked lady's fingers, as we called sponge fingers, and I think Lillian sometimes used strong black coffee to impart a slightly different perfume to the mousse. But this was only if we had eaten it too often and were in danger of becoming jaded. Lillian must have enjoyed baking, as she treated us often to those fruit pies, especially blueberry, that are the real glory of the American kitchen, and pecan pie, the supreme creation of the south.

Plenty of clearance had to be allowed for Lillian to serve at table, and it must have been tiring for her, but she always wanted to serve herself, if only to show how handsome her roast chicken was before it was carved, how brown and crisp the outside of her standing rib roast, and how rare each slice was. Her baked hams, brought to the table whole, glistened with their honey glaze, and there was a whole clove lovingly inserted into each intersection of the diamonds she had scored in the fat. Her *coq au vin* and beef *bourgignon* (though I doubt if we called them by their right names) were at least the equal of Mattie's, her mashed potatoes unequalled until I tasted Joël Robuchon's. Lillian's breadrolls were the lightest, her pastry the flakiest, even her vinaigrette dressing was a revelation.

She refined Lola's recipes, giving us both her fricassee and an authentic *fricassée*; she could do magic with the frozen Gulf shrimp that was all the seafood we had. Her spinach was buttery, and cooked so lightly that each leaf was separate. The mustard and cayenne flavoured, devilled hard-boiled eggs she would prepare for a picnic or cold supper were unlike any I've tasted since.

With such food, naturally, a high standard of decorum was expected, even from the children. We dined seriously at Lola's, which meant formally, with starched white napkins and table cloths, heavy silver cutlery, good china and better table manners. The slightest solecism was instantly detected and pointed out. We weren't expected to sing for our supper; but we were expected to be agreeable – if possible, charming – table companions. At Lola's table, we always tried harder.

Chapter Eight

The sun really did shine bright on my ol' Kentucky home, a little too bright for comfort in the summer. I am afraid I have under-emphasised the skeeters-am-a-hummin'-on-the-honey-suckle-vine aspects of the place. In spring, the whole town was perfumed and made Japanesely pretty by the pink and white of the flowering dogwood, *Cornus florida*, that we can't grow in England because the summer is seldom hot enough to ripen the wood. This wonderful plant can grow to make quite a large tree, and I miss it even more than the large ivory-flowered *Magnolia grandiflorum* with its huge waxy-green leaves. Some gardeners, but not me, can grow this against a south-facing wall in southern England. Kentucky was *hot*. In the stillness of an early summer evening in my childhood, you'd hear nothing but the chirping of crickets, smell nothing but the sickly sweet honeysuckle and see nothing but the stars and the flickering fireflies. That was before the hum of the air-conditioner became the universal night sound. I've returned to Lexington in the summer when the temperature effortlessly topped one hundred degrees on the Fahrenheit thermometer. I was very glad to have lost the song of the skeeters and crickets to the cooling din of the machine.

How did we manage? Indian Mound Road was not air-conditioned the first five years or so of our residence there, although it was a brand-new 'ranch house' when we first took possession of it. How did I survive my new school, Lafayette

Junior High School, in summer? I don't even remember there being overhead fans. I suppose we were just tougher then. I cannot believe the pre-greenhouse-effect world had got that much hotter.

Lafayette Junior High was set in the grounds of the older, larger and more interesting High School itself. As for surviving it, so far as I was concerned, it was dangerously close to Picadome. A few of the Picadome children of the brutalised peasantry and the lumpenproletariat (as I viewed them, but was unable then to name them) did disturb the tranquility of Lafayette Junior High. But not so many as colonised it in the worst of my bad dreams. (There was a vocational school in the same grounds; is it possible that it siphoned off the non-academic children at the early age of twelve? In fact, many of my friends from Kenwick were, like me, bussed south every day; though a few were sent to boarding school for the next three years. For some reason Junior High was thought to be a treacherous academic gap in the Lexington school system. Not for me, it wasn't, for I soon began learning Latin and French. Latin, being a safely moribund language, the pronunciation of which did not matter, was taught as competently as it would be anywhere with a second-rate school system. French was another matter. It was an hilarious, but real case of *bon jour* y'all, in the pretty mouth of the Junior High French teacher who rejoiced in the southern name of Mary Jo. Mary Jo (I didn't call her that, but I've forgotten her surname) had been a dancer, and once appeared in a film – I think Stanley Donen's great *Seven Brides for Seven Brothers*, and after school she gave ballroom dancing lessons in the gym. These were very necessary, we thought at the time, to confer some social graces upon the great unwashed (who were easily in the majority), so they could participate in the 'sock hops' that were now the rage in 1950s teenage America. It was the era of horrid coy songs, such as 'The Naughty Lady of Shady Lane', who, as you will remember was 'only five days old' – or some equally sentimental infantile figure, to which the inadequate antidote were songs like 'Sh-boom, sh-boom', the remainder of whose words were 'da-ya-ta-ta, ta-ta-ta'. Elvis would soon purify teenage music by replacing all this yucky shudder-making nonsense with raunch and sentimentality.

Being sardonic about all this is a way of avoiding the mildly hurtful truth that, in supposedly classless America, there were systematic social divisions that Proust would have taken some getting used to. Southerners, especially, were as worried about the nuances of their position in the pecking order, and about the status of everybody with whom they came into contact, as any character in Jane Austen's novels. I don't imagine Mary Jo knew – not many of the teachers at Lafayette Junior High would have done – but for a whole year before we began school there, almost every single one of the upper-middle-class children had been waltzing, fox-trotting and even jiving the night away at Mrs Hall's School of Dance. For, as in every southern town, there was a parallel set of institutions for the rich or the genteel, whose existence was not even suspected by those further down the social ladder. Admission to Mrs Hall's classes was strictly by invitation, and those invited, nasty little snobs though we might have been, never boasted about it – or even let on – to our uninvited schoolmates. I don't know why we kept Mrs Hall's a secret among ourselves. Perhaps we were afraid of being mocked by those who were excluded. Inclusion was on strict class lines; the fees were affordable by most middle-class parents, and there was no anti-Semitism or anti-Catholic bias. I am writing about the year 1952: of course there were no black children. The schools would remain segregated for another two years, or even more, until the authorities complied with the 1954 Supreme Court ruling. I should not be surprised, though, if there were black children at Mrs Hall's school – or its successor – today. Class, not even colour, was paramount; and I feel sure middle-class Lexington could integrate the children of the black bourgeoisie.

Mrs Hall's classes were quite exciting, for reasons I don't think she ever imagined. One parent would collect a car full of children, bathed and dressed in suits for the boys, dresses, low heels and gloves for the girls. Irv Gail once complained because I smelled of English Leather, the same expensive after-shave he used himself – applied, in my case, as after-bath. We earnestly applied ourselves to learning the steps and the rhythms of the dances of the day, and all the small courtesies the boys were meant to do for the girls, as well as the graces with which the young ladies were meant to return them. In addition to mastering the rhumba, we learnt how to ask for a dance, how to fill in the dance card, how to cut in, when not to do so, and that it was insufferably rude to refuse to dance with anyone. The boys, naturally, made all the running.

We also learnt about sitting out. That was the good bit. You sat out a dance by taking your partner up to the gallery. If, as often happened, there were no parents or chaperones in the gallery that evening, you could have your hand up your partner's dress, inside her bra or her knickers, quicker than Mrs Hall could announce the Viennese waltz. Kissing was out, it could be seen from the dance floor, but even the heaviest petting was undetectable, thanks to Mrs Hall's innocent arrangement of the lights, all of which focused on the action on the dance floor. Quite a few of the girls were amenable to a near-tumble in the gallery. I preferred the company there of my permissive distant cousin, a blonde, glamorous and generously developed twelve-year-old.

Further social hurdles awaited the elect who had made it to Mrs Hall's dancing classes. Most southern towns have an institution called Cotillion – christened after the elaborate dance that, at a time nearer the Civil War, was the chief feature of the organised balls that now bear its name. Lexington Cotillion held about four formal dances a year. It was the old southern precursor of whatever organisation now sponsors the débutante nonsense of the present day. Heaven knows what the ageing socialites who ran it thought its purpose was, but its *raison d'être* would be as plain as the nose on his face to any anthropologist or sociologist. It was a marriage mart: a way of defining who was free to marry whom. The members of Cotillion went in age from fifteen or sixteen to eighteen or so; at the middle of adolescence, then, it set the social boundaries for its members. In effect, it was society saying to you: these are the people your family and their peers have decided are suitable dancing partners for you, and it is from among their number that you shall choose your sexual partner, your husband or wife.

Anthropological speculation apart, membership of Cotillion was concealed from non-members as closely as atomic secrets or membership of the Klan. Nobody ever said to us not to talk out loud about Cotillion. But it was obvious that the Lexington equivalents of Peter Townend, who runs the informal London register of debs and their delights, had pruned the list of Mrs Hall's eligibles ruthlessly. And we avoided talk of Cotillion in front of our friends who hadn't 'made' it out of a natural delicacy that is one of the few things that does any of us any credit. There were few Jews – very few Jews – but there were some.

Cotillion was formal, dinner jackets, white in summer, black the rest of the year for boys, ball gowns for girls. In my time that meant dozens of stiff crinolines supporting acres of taffeta encased in a layer of virtue-protecting tulle. These southern belles would have no problem preserving their virginity – you couldn't get anywhere near their lower halves while they were dressed. And to undress took more than the fifteen minutes or so you could be absent from the dance floor without attracting a chaperone's attention. The chaperones could not, however, prevent us lads from having a quick snorter in the Gents from our hip flasks. So here you have it, real Tennessee Williams stuff – sexual frustration and drunkenness, the essence of the south. The great thing about Cotillion was that you weren't supposed to come with a date. That meant you could leave with one, if you were of driving age (which was sixteen), and her father would trust you with her, and *your* father would trust you with his car.

I don't remember much about Cotillion (probably as a result of too many trips to the Gents), except that the balls were frequently held at the country clubs that did not welcome Jews as members, and that the girls always seemed to have corsages of flowers (given to them by their fathers?) and the boys buttonholes. I'm afraid I do not even recall who the members were in my era. As the dances were held at times convenient for those at boarding school further south or in the east, I presume we had a Whitney or two, and other sprogs of the Thorough-bred aristocracy. Funnily enough, the only girls who come to mind now were the un-identical twin daughters of Garvice Kin-kcad, who was supposed to be the richest man in town, and who had, by the time I am writing about, bought the Richmond Road house from Uncle Louis and Lola. Garvice removed the kennels and put in a swimming pool. Very sensible, I thought.

Life at school bumbled along. We were taught nothing of consequence until the ninth grade, which, at other schools, would have been the 'freshman' year of high school proper; and we retained the vestiges of this system, so that you started learning real subjects, algebra, geometry, history, sciences and languages only then. Biding my time academically, I had singing lessons, in which I learnt to project my voice strongly across a crowded room, a party trick I can still do today and, of course, there was my violin to lose. Once a year the school took part in public speaking competitions, held out of town, at a college somewhere even smaller than Lexington. Though I didn't take part in the debating events, I could be relied upon to win the top marks in all the individual speaking and reading events, as, thanks to my linguistic re-training at Camp Roosevelt, I could iron out my drawl until my speech was perfectly intelligible to most speakers of English. The judges appreciated this ability, though they undoubtedly lacked it themselves. Much more time was spent in imitation of real high school students, 'dating'.

Besides sock hops, there were hayrides on the back of a lorry, strewn with a bale of hay, and taking us to some agrestic destination for a picnic. The great occasion of the school social calendar was the formal dances given by the girls' social clubs, who spent all their after-school free time conducting jumble sales to raise the money to hire a hall and a band and print dance cards.

These clubs were modelled on the older, more established ones of the high school, where the boys, we knew, had 'fraternities', which sounded terribly grown up. In fact, all five or six of these clubs or fraternities existed only for the purpose of raising funds to give a dance once a year; and very often they failed in this. Some or all of the girls' clubs offered membership to Jewish girls, if they were pretty or popular enough, but the fraternities had never admitted a Jewish boy. I so lived in awe, dread and hope of being the first Jewish boy elected to one of them that my judgement was distorted and, with a group of friends, I tried to found a junior high fraternity. We had the full panoply of fraternity rituals and artefacts, including the hazing of younger boys foolish enough to wish to join, and elaborate and expensive silver pins representing the last two letters of the Greek alphabet.

I was obsessed. This was quite a normal state for me; but my obsession now was with conforming. Adolescence had taken over from common sense. I not only wanted to be like the other boys, I wanted to be liked by them; in fact, I insisted on being the most popular child in the school. And I went some way towards realising – even enforcing my demands. In the ninth grade, I took over (probably by hijacking it) the editorship of the school paper and changed it from a Roneo'd to a letterpress printed sheet. I ingratiated myself with nearly everybody by printing, in its last issue, a picture of every ninth grader who was graduating junior high and, in so doing, exceeded the budget so dramatically that the paper folded.

In my pursuit of conformity, I lost my juvenile grip on

reality. I neglected or ignored my real friends, such as Mitch, and forgot about the parallel and grander social life represented by Cotillion. I just wanted to be accepted, as one of themselves, by the ordinary, popular, basketball-playing, WASP, southern American high school boys. That, of course, was out of the question.

The solution was obvious, but I don't know whether it was Murph or me who first thought of boarding school. Lots of Lexington boys (and some girls) were sent east to 'prep' schools; it was quite normal, if your parents had the money and the social nous, to go away for the last three or four years of schooling before college. To be honest, it was the only way to get an education, as Lexington standards were not high. Greek, for example, had fallen into desuetude, and was no longer taught in any of the local schools. Very few offered German. The final year of high school mathematics was, absurdly, solid geometry followed by trigonometry – very useful for those of us who would be plumbers and surveyors. In the redneck, Protestant fundamentalist south, it was even possible to be taught biology, as I was, by a teacher who did not believe in evolution.

So Murph arranged for me to take the entrance exams for Andover and Exeter, then the two best but toughest prep schools in the country. I was pleased to prepare for them, and worked hard, as my head was filled with romantic visions of New England autumns, dormitory life, toasting crumpets on open fires, and other images derived by muddling *Catcher in the Rye* with hundreds of British public school stories. Exeter was in New Hampshire. We visited its spartan facilities when the snow lay two feet thick on the ground. I took fright. Andover, in the more civilised state of Massachusetts, was better, though still chilly. Mitch, we knew, was going to Phillip's Andover Academy (to give it its proper name). Andover normally prepared boys for Harvard; so far as Murph was concerned, it was perfect for me (he had conceded Exeter).

I now regret my subversive interview with the headmaster.

Murph was firmly ushered out of the headmaster's study into an ante-room, leaving me alone with this kindly New England patrician to whom I behaved in an underhanded fashion. Instead of coming out into the open with my ambivalence about leaving home, I conveyed to him the negative side of my feelings. We were ostensibly discussing my programme of studies at Andover. He said that, as my Latin was so strong, I should presumably wish to continue my classics by adding Greek. I countered that he must not judge my prowess at Latin by the marks I had got for the subject at my school, or even by the fact that I had come high in the competitive examinations. Latin, I said, was so badly taught, and studied by so few other students, that the fact that I was one of the best Latin students in Lexington was quite meaningless. I should not be surprised, I went on, if I needed remedial work merely to catch up with the standard of Latin as taught at Andover. He got the point of my unwonted humility. Shortly after we returned to Lexington, we got a telegram from the headmaster of Andover, explaining that there had been a mix-up about the number of beds or spaces available in the dormitories and that, much to his chagrin, there would, after all, be no room for me at Andover in the coming academic year. Murph was astonished, but if he suspected my defection, he never let on.

I got myself expelled from Andover without ever having been a student there, because I had acquired a new interest in Lexington, or, to be more precise, a new obsession. I was besotted by a boy I shall call Barry. I had known Barry in the sixth grade, but then his parents sent him away to school, to one of those peculiar southern military academies, a junior version of the sort of place where Marlon Brando went so odd in *Reflections in a Golden Eye*. His Bible-thumping parents (evangelical Christians had been in the habit of being born again for decades before renascence caught on in the rest of the USA) could not have suspected that they were sending their eldest child to a school whose traditions were drawn from those of the Royal Navy, but *mutatis mutandis*, most of what Barry learnt at military school had to do with rum, sodomy and the lash.

Barry charmed everybody. I cannot think why. He was of only medium intelligence, pathetically skinny and his face was acne'd, no doubt because of an excess of the male sex hormones that made him perpetually randy. He certainly charmed me: our relationship began by my helping him with his Latin homework, and then virtually doing it for him for a year until he gave up the subject. We spent a lot of time chasing girls and, after a fashion, succeeded in catching them – usually in the cheap seats of the sleaziest of the local cinemas. We knew girls like these were no better than they should be, and worried, after touching them – and each other – up, whether you could catch syphilis or the clap this way. It seemed all too likely.

Barry wanted to fuck everything that moved but, in 1950s America, even his powers of persuasion were too feeble to overcome the virginity-mania and mortal fear of pregnancy that were the twin behaviour axioms of every nice girl – and of most of the cinema sluts as well. Though I learnt years later that he had solicited sexual favours from another of our schoolmates, Barry wasn't homosexual, just dynamically, overwhelmingly, explosively horny. As we might have guessed from the entertaining goings-on of the Swaggarts and Bakkers of the world, there seems to be an intrinsic connection between extreme evangelical beliefs and extreme randiness, so maybe Barry's Bible-bashing background was responsible for his priapism.

Though his family moved once or twice in the course of our friendship, Barry was never far away from my own house. Which was a good thing, for as my obsession with him grew, so did the compulsion to know his whereabouts, and I would zoom over on my bicycle to his house three or four times in a single post-school afternoon. Our parents, different as chalk and cheese, never met socially; but his were well off enough, and lived in a grand enough house, to reassure my parents that he was unlikely to lead me too far astray. Little did they know.

We were allowed to stay at each other's house occasionally, though Barry was more welcome at mine than I was at his. Besides cheating at Latin and mutual masturbation, we drank and smoked cigarettes. His tee-total parents would have collapsed in stunned despair had they known of our depravities, and I cannot think how Babe and Shirley failed to notice the falling level of booze in the Bourbon bottle, or smell the Lucky Strike-perfumed air of my bedroom. Most of our time together was spent in plotting to get laid. Or rather, in having fantasies about it; for though Lexington was meant to be well-stocked with brothels, neither of us had a clue where any of them might be. Nor did we know any prostitutes. And though we entertained ourselves with endless speculations about which of the girls we knew was the likeliest to oblige, we damned well knew that there was a stronger possibility of losing our virginity to Doris Day than to any of the high school girls.

Years later at university I realised that my obsession with Barry had parallels in my current neurotic behaviour. But when Dr Kavka remarked, almost casually, that I had been in love with Barry, I was genuinely shocked. Perhaps I was. I hadn't thought of it that way.

Besides girls, Barry and I shared another constant goal – to have a car. I was the older, and by the minimum legal age of sixteen, urged on by Barry (though it wasn't necessary; only wimps failed to get their driving licences as young as possible), I passed my test. As soon as possible after that, I borrowed the family car, a classic, Raymond Loewy-designed, 1951 Studebaker, on every possible pretext, and went joy-riding or trawling for girls with Barry.

One day in early summer, I was persuaded by Barry to take the car, laden with water-skis, and one younger brother each, way out on the Richmond Road, to the Kentucky River at Boonesborough, where he had access to a power boat. I knew Shirley would never agree to me driving such a distance and, though I was on the whole truthful, I told a lie direct about our destination. (I think I said we were going to Joyland.) She would also have objected because the road, the continuation of the road so daringly traversed earlier by my grandfather's pick-up truck, was notoriously dangerous.

We went to the river. We water-skied – the only time I have done so in my life and we smoked whole packets of cigarettes. I do not think we drank any alcohol. We were later than we ought to have been. We hurried back to Lexington, with speed-freak Barry in the seat-beltless front passenger seat urging me to accelerate even more, and lighting cigarettes and placing them between my lips. I don't know how fast we were going when we left the road, flew down an embankment and hit a very large tree. Only my brother, asleep on the back seat, was not injured. The local newspaper printed a front-page photograph of the wrecked car with the details of its occupants. It was meant to serve as a warning to the yobbos; what could not happen to them, if the children of some of the town's leading citizens could so misbehave?

Lying in my hospital bed with both legs in plaster, one of them suspended in the air in traction, I reaped the rewards of the publicity: several anonymous, illiterate letters from girls who said they were passionately in love with me. I also made medical history by catching a severe case of poison ivy in hospital. At least I gave every appearance of having done so. It is probable that I landed in a patch of the vicious herb when the impact of the crash propelled me half out of the car. The huge, painful water blisters of the poison ivy had their uses; they took my guilt-ridden mind off the pains in the shattered femur of my right leg, the two broken ankle bones of the left leg, the neck injury, broken nose and injury to the right elbow. The surgeons only concerned themselves with the first two, which I have to admit were dramatic enough. When the morphine injections didn't ease the pain, the nurse blamed it on the poison ivy; I was paranoid, probably because of the morphine, and accused the nurses of giving me placebo injections of water. Stalemate. But the mad, nearly surreal quality of it made us all able to laugh about it later.

At first Barry's injuries were thought to be worse than my own. I didn't attempt to blame him for what happened, though I expected his parents, at least, to see all the fault as lying with me. Shirley was wonderful. In a real crisis she was strong. Though Murph brooded and whinged a bit, and was obviously angry, Shirley never reproached me for anything except for lying about the destination of our doomed joy-ride. Babe was kind; so was Shirley's brother, Uncle Manuel Singer, who had met the ambulance on arrival at hospital and bravely prevented a power-crazed cop from turning me over on my stretcher to get at my driver's licence in the wallet in my inaccessible back pocket. I soon learnt who my friends were too. Real friends were not put off by my act of juvenile delinquency (as we labelled such misdeeds then), or too embarrassed at the prospect of having to talk about it to bring themselves to visit me in hospital. Many were, of course. But I shall never forget that Mike Ades, at a different school and a little older than me, visited me every day, talked to me without lugubriousness or solemnity, and kept up my morale, to the point where I could at least entertain the thought that I had been unlucky as well as wicked.

For along with the poison ivy, I had caught in hospital a little of the religion of Barry's parents. I was deeply worried that Barry was going to die of his injuries, and I tried to prevent this by praying. Of course I didn't know any prayers – or even how to pray. I only knew how to mumble quite meaningless words in Hebrew, which were mostly, as near as I could remember any of the English translations on the facing page of the prayerbook, about how goodly Jacob's tents were. Though I knew by heart, from listening to the radio on Sunday nights, the entire contents of the Methodist and Southern Baptist hymnals, I could not see how Barry would be aided in his plight by my singing or reciting 'The Old Rugged Cross' or 'I walked in the garden alone,/ while the dew was still on the ro- ses,' which was all I then understood of the religion of his parents. My morbid religious phase was over when Barry's symptoms disappeared.

No wonder. Barry had suffered a compound fracture of the femur of one leg, and the wound simply would not heal sufficiently to allow the doctors to perform the standard operation that would mend the fracture in a matter of weeks. I don't know why it never occurred to any of them or to Barry's nurses that the problem was that he was constipated.

In my private room, further along the corridor in the Good Samaritan Hospital, we seldom thought about anything else. I had a single ambition for my stay in hospital: to avoid the attentions of Sweet Evening Breeze.

Sweet Evening Breeze ('Sweets,' for short, and we talked about him so often we had need of a shortened form) was a black transvestite, a legend among Lexington's schoolboy population. He worked as an orderly at the hospital, doing menial jobs, among which the chief was that he administered the enemas. Or so we believed. Rumour had it that he was allowed to wear a specially designed uniform, with a large floppy collar, that set him apart from the other male orderlies, and placed him, ambiguously, in the company of the female nurses' aides. It was also said that if he took a fancy to you, he'd bake a chocolate cake and bring it to you following a successful enema. It was moreover claimed that he had gone through a sort of marriage ceremony with another man, and that he had looked wonderful in his bridal gown. For once, every word of the schoolboy gossip was true.

In *The Blue Hen's Chick*, A. B. Guthrie jnr, the 'local colourist' who was Lexington's most popular and probably best known novelist, wrote a portrait of Sweet Evening Breeze, from which I learnt that his real name was James Herndon, that 'his small house, which he himself kept, was immaculate, said those who knew, and furnished tastefully with antiques. He was known as an excellent cook, of pastries particularly.' Guthrie continued: 'James was effeminate in movement, response and, to a degree, dress. His voice was light, his walk short-stepped and mannered. He liked to groom himself and in public to appear in clean, pressed hospital whites. Once he was the featured performer as reported in Colored Notes [a column in the local newspaper], in a Negro extravaganza. Lowered in a basket from the ceiling of the Woodland Auditorium, decked out in feminine frills, he danced the Passion Dance of the Bongo Bangoes. I regret that I didn't see it.' Me, too.

'It came to pass,' Guthrie relates, 'by the sworn word of witnesses, that in the days of Dud Veal as City Detective, James was brought to the station house for an offence, imagined or real. One of Dud's fellow sleuths was Joe Harrigan, who was a shade the more literate.

'Dud took the arrest blotter and laboriously began making the entry. Then he looked up at Harrigan. "I don't know what to book him for," he said.

'Harrigan chewed on a cigar and sized up James. "Book him," he said, "for bein' a goddam proverb."'

As for the story of Sweet Evening Breeze's wedding, I have in front of me a black and white snapshot. It shows him in a white wedding dress, with white gloves to the elbow, a long train, and a veil pulled back to reveal a long neck and a youthful-looking oval face. He is standing in a garden and carrying an enormous bouquet of flowers.

After I had been in hospital four or five days, Sweet Evening Breeze made a dramatic entrance into my room, striking a Mae West pose in the doorway. I was more than alarmed. Terror gripped my heart and, more to the point, fear seized my bowels. Sweets was known to like blonds. My private nurse, seeing my eyes filled with fright at this cross-dressed apparition, was so overcome by mirth that she had to smother her laughter in her handkerchief and run out into the hall for relief.

The spectre in drag went away, leaving me to beg the nurse for prune juice, well known to schoolboys for its laxative effects. In a panic, I drank glass after glass. I finished the bottle. It was only a matter of hours until it worked. It kept on working. Bedpan followed bedpan. I had given myself diarrhoea. The houseman was called by the overworked nurse. I scarcely heard their conversation, except when he departed, promising that help was on its way.

A few minutes later, framed in the doorway of my room, Sweet Evening Breeze was grinning. He carried with him the sinister implements of his calling. I had never before heard of using a high enema to cure the squitters, but that's what the doctor had ordered. It was even more uncomfortable than I had imagined. I had no dignity left when Sweets appeared the next day with the cake; I thanked him warmly and offered a slice to the nurse. In no time at all he had cured Barry, who was soon out of hospital.

I took longer. For ten months I was in a hospital bed, mostly at home, looked after at first by nurses, then by Shirley and, I think, Mary Elizabeth, who had had hospital experience with psychiatric patients. The very best teachers in the school had agreed to come to my bedside and tutor me privately, and thus I did Latin, French and Euclidean geometry. I was so adeptly mobile with my wheelchair that I could get myself out of bed and on to the loo unassisted. I could even have opened the front door, but I was never left alone to do so, except, oddly, once when Barry was brought for a visit in his wheelchair. He was soon released from it and back to school on crutches. I pined for him, but his parents had decided that I was the corrupter, and we were not allowed to see each other again. When we did next meet, on the day I returned to school all those months later, there was an emotional frost.

I wasn't too hurt. I'd grown up a lot in those months of near-solitude, in which I'd found the patience to take hours making model boats and aeroplanes, and read every book in the house, from Hemingway and Steinbeck to Christopher Fry (why was Shirley reading *him*?) and a great deal of rubbish. Visitors soon learnt that the best way to please me was to bring me a work of current fiction. Accordingly, I made my way through the works of John Masters, James Gould Cozzens and J. P. Marquand. Shirley tolerantly bought me *Peyton Place* and *The Man in the Grey Flannel Suit*. Nobody tried to improve my mind, thank God.

The plaster was removed, and I expected to be in the leather and metal leg braces that replaced them for at least a year, maybe more. The orthopaedic surgeons had done a brilliant job. I learnt that, in order to save the right leg, they had performed an original and radical operation, which involved the insertion of two titanium plates at right angles to each other, a short one anchored to the knee, the longer perpendicular one fastened by screws to the few shards of bone that remained of the femur. (I only once had occasion again to see an orthopaedic surgeon, an eminent Harley Street man; on seeing the X-rays he had ordered, he named the pair of Lexington surgeons who had operated on me, and said it was their work as clearly as though they had signed it.) Nobody had any idea how or at what rate the bone would grow back. Ten months after the initial operation, while I was still in a wheelchair, and only practising standing up with crutches to learn balance again, a routine X-ray showed a strong cladding of bone around the long plate. Showing a robust sense of drama, the doctor told me to rise up from the X-ray table and walk. I crossly thought he was teasing me, so I did it. Shirley almost fainted.

The day I was told I could walk without the braces, Shirley made me drive the car home. It was a supreme vote of confidence.

Chapter Nine

In spring, 1958 I went back to school. Almost immediately Norma Wikler became the most important person in my life. She had embarked on a programme to disrupt and then take over the school, and she had need of a trustworthy lieutenant.

Norma, who was pretty alarming in prospect, is altogether amazing in retrospect. As a schoolgirl, she determined to be a dancer despite her large, gawky frame, and to be a flautist, in spite of her tone-deafness. She was perfectly right: will-power more than made up for the absence of the conventional qualifications for entrée to the ballet and orchestra. Norma came to collect me a couple of years ago from my room at San Francisco's smartest hotel; her bottled-blonde hair was smartly cut to call attention to her high cheek-bones; she was wearing stiletto heels that made her nearly six feet tall, and her svelte model's body was encased in a sexy, shiny rubber raincoat with fastenings in odd places. Norma shrieked with laughter on entering my room. She was certain that the hall porter had thought she was a tart who specialised in rubber fetishes, and that I was her client.

Professor Norma Wikler, now of the University of California at Santa Cruz, and advisor to the judiciary of several of the United States and Canada, was the second of the four children of Abraham Wikler, a distinguished neuro-pharmacologist who had come to Lexington to work at the Federal Narcotics institution that we all called Narco. For many years, any prominent person convicted of drug-using offences in a Federal court would be given a choice of going to prison or coming to Lexington for treatment by Abe Wikler and his colleagues.

Young Norma profited from her father's job — literally. Narco was in rural surroundings — we used to call it the narcotics farm. Norma would ride her pony around the fenced perimeter, stopping and collecting small parcels along the way. These she handed in to the guards, who paid her a bounty of ten cents for each package. She now admits that she knew that these were the inmates' dope supplies, hurled over the fence by their confederates in the town, and that the guards were running the racket, selling the drugs to the actresses and jazz musicians who would otherwise have been suffering the cold turkey treatment. Norma can't think how she was silly enough, even at the age of six or eight, to have settled for only ten cents.

Abe Wikler's hobby was learning languages. He especially relished the non-Indo-European ones. He was prodigiously clever, but not a good judge of his children's abilities. Convinced that Norma, if not thick, was the least bright of his four children, he refused to believe that she was academic material. The eldest, Margie, was sent to what Abe was persuaded was the best university in America, the University of Chicago. (He insisted that I apply for admission there too, as he did not want me to waste my time, as he saw matters, at Harvard.) A mathematician, Margie got her Ph.D. when she was ludicrously young. She had agreed with her supervisor to write about a particular problem well known to people in her field, and the solution came to her while she was in the bath, only a few days after the topic had been assigned.

Margie was bold. With a friend, she went to one of Billy Graham's evangelical 'crusades' out of curiosity, and decided to be converted for the fun of it. She was impressed by the expert, efficient and expensive back-up organisation. As soon as she stepped forward to bear witness for Christ, she was whisked away and made to fill in a sort of census form. In a trice she was matched up with a spiritual advisor as like herself as possible: white, female, young, college-educated, but not, of course, sceptical and Jewish. Her sister-in-God put her back into the new-born Christian's conversion, and Margie hallelujah'd away with her for the rest of the evening, very much enjoying her experience of salvation. Margie knew that the Billy Graham organisation was certain to remain in daily touch with her; having gained her soul, they would not be likely to lose it through inattention. She said she felt quite sorry for the enemy whose name, address and telephone number she had given.

After Norma, came Dan, the only boy, who is now a professor of philosophy, specialising in medical ethics. The youngest Wikler child, Jean, after studying mime with Marcel Marceau, settled in Holland, where she makes films and has in the past had her own television chat show – in Dutch. I often cite her case to people who are worried by the absence of Lexington in my speech.

Norma was allowed a certain amount of freedom when she was still at school. While I was on my back making model aeroplanes and reading Marcel Pagnol with my French tutor, Norma was in Paris, ostensibly learning to speak French. What she was in fact doing was unintentionally participating in riots for Algerian independence. Norma has always insisted she was a mere spectator of the demonstrations culminating in the one that, *l'Humanité* claimed, involved one million protestors. One day, though, watching a demo somewhere near Sainte Germain des Prés, Norma took fright when she saw the police use their clubs on members of the crowd. She ran away from the scene of the violence, down the rue Bonaparte, and didn't stop for breath or turn around until she had run into a little restaurant she knew and out the back door. Norma was surprised and not pleased to see that she had been followed by hundreds and hundreds of demonstrators who were now pouring out of the back entrance of the bistro.

This was the elemental force Abe Wikler was trying to subdue when he decided Norma wasn't smart enough to do an ordinary undergraduate course, and sent her to train as a nurse. Norma ended up with a doctorate in medical sociology, and is the only person I have ever known who has sold the film rights to her Ph.D. thesis. (To Jane Fonda. The dissertation was about drug addiction among Vietnam war veterans.)

All those years ago, Norma and I had performed the miracle of the moving forsythia at Sunday school. Now, under her direction, we set about subverting Lafayette High School. I think Norma's family was probably left-wing by Lexington standards, though I never really knew anything about Abe Wikler's views. It was the end of the McCarthy period, and even if you owned them, you didn't leave the volumes of the Little Lenin Library sitting about on shelves where they could be seen. But our sabotage was more social than political, in any case. Whatever the ruling order, we should have been against it. We were junior nihilists in the style of those in Dostoevsky's *The Possessed* – as it appeared to us several years later when we'd read the book.

Our glorious careers began with Norma taking over the school newspaper, with me, I suppose, as her deputy.

The 1954 Supreme Court order was at last being implemented in Fayette County and Lafayette High School was being integrated. To get the full flavour of this, you need a little background. The school song went: 'Winding driveways lead us upwards/ To the summit of the hill,/ Where in beauty facing forwards/ Lafayette's walls our dreams fulfill./ Home of lofty thought and learning,/ Beacon o'er the Meadowland,/ Shrine whence still the ever-burning/ Torch is passed from hand to hand.' This hilarious and topographically inaccurate mangling of the city-on-the-hill theme was sung to the tune of *Deutschland über Alles*, and had been adopted as the school anthem, Norma and I reckoned, sometime during the Second World War. (There was no excuse: 'Glorious things of thee are spoken' was not sung much in Lexington churches, and 'Vienna' did not figure greatly in the evangelical churches' hymnals.)

Was there resistance to integrating the school racially? To be honest, I don't remember any. But there had been a cross-burning on the front lawn, and in Norma's favourite fantasy a high official of the school had been there, dancing around it, hidden in a white sheet. There weren't many black kids; at first only two girls to several hundred whites. Norma and I, of course, wrote editorials demanding good treatment for them. I don't recall anybody actually treating them badly; and as I have no recollection of either of their names, I don't expect Norma and I went out of our way to make friends of them. Revolutionaries don't have time to be sentimental.

Despising as we did the traditional values that made the football and basketball players the school heroes, and the elevated status of their molls, the cheerleaders in their short skirts and tight sweaters (which more often revealed under-development than voluptuously generous bosoms – cheerleader style being more Doris Day than Jane Russell), we set about a programme of subtle, but systematic denigration of them. We complained about the poor qualities of their intellects. We said in editorials that higher grade standards ought to be required of those who got 'letters' in their sports; that athletes, and certainly cheerleaders, should not be excused academic study periods to practise their sports or their choreography. We wrote pompous, but learned pieces on the purposes of education.

Finally, as was inevitable, we exceeded the mark. We published an editorial, written by me I should think, condemning the bad spelling of the 'Pep Club' posters. These, stuck up all over the building, inexpertly lettered and crudely drawn by hand, either advertised the next home football or basketball match, or, with equal frequency, exhorted attendance at a rally, to be led by the cheerleaders, for the purpose of inspiring the members of one of the teams to achieve victory. It was one thing for Norma and me to write Nigger-loving editorials, or to pummel the broad shoulders of the athletes; it was quite another to attack the spelling abilities of the Pep Club members. The Pep Club, you see, consisted of girls too fat, too ugly, too unpopular and (if it was possible) too stupid to be cheerleaders. They were the lump of High School society. They were already down – as low down as you could get – argued the school authorities. How could we have been so cruel to people so wretched?

Norma was sacked. I, naturally, resigned in protest. So did the sports editor and the photographer, leaving, I think, nobody with enough experience to put out the paper. That was my last brush with journalism (except for a short-lasting flirtation with my college newspaper) for nearly twenty years.

Shortly after this we went by coach on a class outing to Cincinnati to see a touring company version of *Music Man*. I am almost sure I have got the details of this right, as I can shut my eyes and see a hundred-and-one-trombones leading the big parade. I was already a snob where Broadway musicals were concerned. Nothing but the prospect of a day away from school could have induced me to be present at a performance of such a trivial show. It was dark in the coaches on the way back, and none of the teachers would have been the wiser about our behaviour had we not been shopped by some of the other students. The Principal said the next day that he could have tolerated the necking, even though it was reported to have been noisy; but he could not overlook the drink. Then, reflecting on the Pep Club incident, his mood turned dark and he said he felt Norma and I were trying to get him fired. He was, he said, in a dilemma. We were two of the best students of our year – no, of the entire school. Why, he was counting on me to be the first pupil Lafayette had ever got into Harvard. He couldn't expel us, it was out of the question; besides, he admitted, our parents were influential, and capable of making trouble. As against this, there was his own position to consider. What would happen to him if the School Board learnt that he was turning a blind eye to our corrupting an entire schoolbus full of young people in a sex and booze scandal? He was pleading with us for his own job. However, he was not asking much – only discretion. We were to leave his office today, unpunished and even unchastised. But we were to keep our noses clean and our heads down.

So we devoted ourselves to other pursuits. There was the world IQ test record to break, for example. A team of psychologists had moved into the school. They were from the university, and they were testing a test that was being hailed as a replacement for the Stanford-Binet IQ test. I'd taken that one often, but we had to take it again as a control. My score was 140. Norma wouldn't tell me hers. I don't know why they told us our scores at all. Maybe it was the price of our co-operation. In any case, we didn't actually believe them. Perhaps we were not entirely confident of the competence of the University of Kentucky graduate students who were testing us. It took about two days to do the new test, which required the person administering it to time lots of things with a stopwatch; and generally to participate in the examination itself. For example, there was one bit of the test that involved cubes, each face of which was bisected into different coloured triangles. Working against the clock, the examinee was shown a card with a coloured geometrical pattern, which he had to duplicate by assembling four of the cubes. I was amazed to find that, each time I was given this test, I only had to alter slightly the position of a single cube to achieve the desired pattern. By the fourth time I did it, I nearly beat the chap who was clicking the stopwatch. I don't think the inventors of this test had quite taken into account these particular random effects, which must have been partly responsible for my ludicrous score of 169.

To Norma I confessed my disappointment. Hadn't Leopold and Loeb, the Nietszche-inspired child-murderers, got IQ scores of around 200? Though we were sufficiently self-aware to know that we were only posing, and though irony and self-mockery were the linchpins of the style we were manufacturing for ourselves, we were nothing if not ambitious. Too bad we didn't know about camp; it was a mode of behaviour that wasn't yet available to us. It would have been very congenial to Norma and me, though I expect we should have lost our already bewildered supporters even sooner.

In our last or senior year of school, the powers-that-be made a drastic, and from the school administration's point of view, almost lethal error. The school was streamed – by ability. This meant that Norma and I and our dozen or so co-conspirators were together in nearly every class. Overnight the quality of the teaching improved, probably as the result of giving the existing teachers their heads. It was well-known that the chemistry teacher was wizard; now, with all the best seniors gathered in a single group, she really pushed the boat out. She compressed into one term the entire contents of the high school chemistry syllabus; in the second term she taught us elementary organic chemistry. Even I, who was considered too poor at maths to have taken the previous year's physics course, was encouraged to take the national College Board examinations, and actually scored a more than creditable 650 out of a perfect 800. We adored the chemistry lab; our small group was there even during the lunch break, most days, frying chips over the Bunsen burners, and mixing up batches of black-powder based paste that exploded on contact. This we used to paint the floor of one of the English classrooms while the teacher was at lunch. When the students shuffled into their desks and chairs after the break, there was a series of satisfying bangs, and the air of the classroom was heavy with sulphurous smoke.

Though I really was bad at maths, there had been a weird

episode the year before, while I was taking my advanced algebra examination. In the course of doing the equations, I began to get very hot, and to develop oedema or hives, very itchy and bothersome. They grew progressively in the course of the two hours or so of the test, and eventually the borders between the spots disappeared and they merged into one giant swelling. Fidgeting, I had removed a shoe at the beginning of the period. When I had finished writing the paper, I could not get it back on. I was allowed to borrow a friend's car and drive myself to our family doctor. On seeing my condition, he rushed me to an allergist, Dr Maurice Kaufmann. Maurie did a few tests, but then decided there was no time to wait, and gave me the first of many injections of adrenalin. He warned me that he had to put a time limit on waiting for the drug to work and that, if it did not work by then, I should have to go to hospital for the equivalent of a 'blue baby' operation, a total exchange of blood by transfusion. By this time I was feeling the exciting effects of the drug; I was detached and unworried. I was high. By questioning me while we were waiting, Maurie found out that I had had an injection of penicillin four or five days earlier. Later tests seemed to confirm that penicillin was the culprit. (Still later experience proved it, as when at Harvard in the late sixties, my un-house-trained puppy was taking a course of the antibiotic; I cleaned up after he had widdled, and my hands and face blew up with oedema, simply from contact with the minute quantity of penicillin excreted in his urine. And yes, I had washed my hands.) The next day the algebra teacher announced that, to her own considerable surprise, I had got the best mark in the examination.

Norma always relished this story, citing it as the ultimate triumph of mind over matter, and bringing it up when, as she frequently felt, she had reason to rebuke me for feebleness. In the course of our term of organic chemistry we were taught the use of the Petri dish for growing organisms in an agar-agar medium. I attempted to culture some fast-growing bacterium, whose cell-division I hoped we should be able to watch under the microscope. Or something like that. Norma was uncharacteristically silent about her 'organism' until, one day, she invited me to watch as she lifted the lid from her Petri dish. She bade me approach as close as possible, which I trustingly did. There was a look of the crazed scientist about her, a complicated set of facial gestures that she must have learnt from careful observation of Jerry Lewis films. I shied away, just as she answered my question, 'What are you growing?' and unveiled her spores, cackling, 'Penicillin.' Norma could be dangerous.

If putting our intellectual élite together for chemistry had turned us into terrorist pranksters, when we were all together for senior English we were transformed into the Waffen-SS. We had met our *Führer*, the senior English master, Donn (with two 'n's) Hollingsworth. He was the great teacher some children are lucky enough to encounter when they're still young enough for someone strange and remarkable, but in a position of great authority, to make an impression. I did not then and do not now know what explained his foibles, or what motivated him to expend his great energies in teaching the English literature that he loved to unlettered and indifferent children. Surely it would have been a bit less frustrating to have taught at the university – though I have to admit that the standards prevailing at the University of Kentucky in the mid-50s were probably not that much higher than those at our academically unambitious high school.

On the first day of class, Holly said: 'By tomorrow you will have memorised the first eighteen lines of the Prologue to *Canterbury Tales*. In Middle English.' If it hadn't been so cruel, nothing would have been funnier than hearing that bunch of bright, but drawling group of seventeen-year-olds struggling to twist their tongues around 'Whan that Aprille with his Showres Soote . . . that hem hath holpen whan that they were seke.' I can still recite it. But the next day I had only learnt nine lines. I made quite a good stab at the pronunciation, too, and the class was flatteringly awe-hushed for my performance, or rather, my half-performance. 'Well, go on, boy,' demanded Holly in his most frightening Dickens schoolmaster's voice. When I confessed I couldn't, he snorted disapproval, and passed on to the next person in the alphabet. His progress was rapid: I was the only one who could manage more than a couplet. 'There is continuous assessment in this classroom,' said Holly, menacing us with the notebook in which he recorded the marks, and it begins today. Everyone of you is starting out with *two* failing marks, except for Levy, who only gets one.'

We were made to read the plays, and memorise whole speeches from Shakespeare. Some days I read Macbeth, some days Duncan; I even had a turn at being Lady Macbeth. We committed to heart 'Tomorrow, and tomorrow and tomorrow', 'I have lived long enough ... the sear, the yellow leaf ... ', 'Is this a dagger which I see before me, the handle toward my hand?' and 'Eye of newt', as well as 'Out, damned spot!' When we did *Julius Caesar, Lear, Hamlet* and *Othello*, Holly no longer told us which passages we were to memorise: 'You ought to be able to judge for yourselves by now.' We were tested on them, however, and marked, just the same. It was a wonderful game, while it lasted. Which passages to memorise from *Hamlet* was dead obvious; *Othello* only a little trickier; *Lear* was a bugger.

Holly gave Shakespeare about a month of our time. It must have been during our reading of one of the comedies that Holly said of some detail of the plot, 'Hmm, reminds me of the Sacco and Vanzetti case. Who can tell me about Sacco and Vanzetti? Levy? You've never *heard* of Sacco and Vanzetti? Get up, boy. The library is on this floor. There are forty minutes left in this period. You have thirty minutes to learn *everything* about the Sacco and Vanzetti case, and come back and explain it to us.'

I did it. Nicola Sacco (b.1891) anarchist and radical agitator born in Italy, executed in 1927 with Bartolomeo Vanzetti (b.1888), after a trial that caused world-wide ructions. 'Not bad, boy. Except you missed the point. They were *innocent*.'

Hollingsworth always rewarded ingenuity, which he seemed to value highly. He taught us the use of documentation, and didn't seem to mind at all when, shortly afterwards, I discovered its abuses. 'Always cite an authority,' was the great rule, but Holly did not preach scrupulosity as to the quality of the sources. I saw this flaw almost immediately, and exploited it. I invented an all-purpose authority, Professor Carruthers. Carruthers was an expert on everything, from proto-Indo-European to ballistics, and I myself was remarkable for having memorised various passages from Carruthers' works, which I was able to quote at impressive length. Holly rumbled this the second or third time Carruthers made an appearance in a 'research' paper written at home. But he evidently approved of this small deceit, and raised no objection when Carruthers was cited even in examinations that were written in the classroom. Professor Carruthers' views on the authorship of Shakespeare, by the way, were ridiculous; but nobody ever seemed to notice that either.

Holly was himself studying at one of the local theological seminaries. There were dozens of them; we were almost in the middle of the Bible Belt, and there was a seminary for every sect – I doubt not for the hillbilly snake-handlers of eastern Kentucky and for our own home-grown charismatics, who could be heard speaking with tongues any old Sunday night – and their babble must have been genuine glossolalia because the town was dry on Sundays – it was illegal to buy or sell drink.

His theological interests, however, were more intellectual: 'Levy, what happened to Origen's testicles, and why? Oh, and you can deal with Abelard while we're on the subject of balls.' Another day: 'Tell us all about Manicheanism, Levy.' 'Now,

Levy, why was Pelagius wrong?' 'Tell me, Levy, whatever became of our local Albigensian heretics?'

Then there'd be a sudden change of tack. 'What do you know about game theory, Levy? Who was John von Neumann? I'll tell you what, you make it your business to find out everything there is to know about him, and you can make it into a long essay for your term paper.' I did just that. I found a long piece on the mathematical-logician in *Time* or *Life* magazine, and ripped it off. I added a picture of my new hero for good measure, reproduced extremely poorly on an early copying machine. 'Nice presentation, Levy. I like people who take a bit of trouble. We'll give you A+ for the semester.'

At least Holly had bothered to mark the paper himself. One day he said, 'You are meant to be the smartest kids in the school. It's a waste of my time grading your papers. You can grade each other's. Here, pass them around, and mark the one on the top of the pile.' From then on, we sat in random judgement on each other. As there was the right of appeal to Holly, no one ever dared to give me less than A; though I once attempted to give Norma a B. She threatened to put a contract out on me, or something equally hideous, and I relented.

It was impossible to tell what Holly really believed, if anything. Possibly, he was, as we fancied ourselves, just a born subversive. He made us read *1984*, *Animal Farm* and *Brave New World* on the one hand, and Ayn Rand's *Atlas Shrugged* on the other. These books were dangerous in combination, for from this literary cocktail Norma and I derived an ideology of egoistic hedonism (for us) and to-hell-with-the-Proles ruthlessness (for everybody else). From Ayn Rand we took away a view that the world is divided into superior and inferior beings, and that the world is there for the enjoyment of the superior, who ought to take their pleasure without feeling any guilt about the miseries of the inferior creatures. (It *does* sound a little like Margaret Thatcher's views when put this way.)

From Huxley and Orwell we learnt how to identify the under-class of epsilons and Proles. It was a joke, of course; self-mocking and full of irony, we thought, as we led our Storm Troops into Holly-sanctioned parties we called 'orgies', and plotted our latest anti-Prole prank.

Not only did we paint explosives under the desks of the Proles (by definition, incidentally – everybody except us and our lieutenants were Proles), we once went one better in Holly's classroom. We made a single elegant construction of all the chairs and desks, including Holly's own, in the room, using a ladder to make sure the last one was wedged firmly against the ceiling. All in the course of a single lunch break. 'Very industrious,' commented Holly, who found it hugely funny.

Another time he was in reflective mood. He sometimes referred to his family; we knew he had a son or brother called Denzil, and he put some effort into convincing us that there were family members called Hrothgar, Horsa and Hengist. He sometimes, in an elaborate literary tease, seemed to mean his wife when he spoke of Beowulf's dam. 'Do you know what it's like being married?' he moaned this particular afternoon. 'Same face on the pillow next to you for all eternity. Covered in white greasy cold cream; and on top of that a mass of metal curlers. Touching you, another body, in competition for space on the mattress that sags towards the centre. The top always left off the toothpaste tube,' and, warming to his theme, 'long hairs, not your own, blocking the drain of the sink. A ring of filth left around the bath tub, for you to clean before you have your own bath' and so on. Then a change. 'My wife', whom he had just finished slandering, 'and I would like you all to come to a party on Saturday in our barn. No hard liquor, and nobody's to get pregnant.'

Nobody ever did get pregnant at any of our 'orgies'. Well, not on the premises, anyway. One or two weak-minded girls (Norma and I said to ourselves, disclaiming any guilt in the matter), might have got over-excited by the glamour of our exclusive parties, and then been stupid with one of the football players somewhere else. What really happened at our orgies, which were generally held at one of our own houses at the weekend when we could be certain that the parents would be out for the whole evening, was that we stole and drank our parents' booze, smoked cigarettes, danced to Elvis records and talked contemptuously of the Proles. The entire reason for having 'wild' parties was to exclude the Proles, and, indeed, it wasn't long before members of the football and basketball teams and other low forms of life were begging admission to our orgies. We had already subverted most of the cheerleaders.

School ended with a 'Class Day', in which those who were about to graduate wore costumes and were allowed to take liberties with the teachers and younger students. Bad hats to the last, we chose 'the Cuban Revolution' as the theme of our carnival day. With that, we brought our guerrilla war against the school into the open.

About half-way through our senior year, I began to realise, with feelings of glee, that I was unfitted to do any practical job for which there was any demand by society. It was a revelation I welcomed, and shared with Norma – who by now didn't mind what she was going to be, so long as she didn't end up being a nurse. She agreed with me, I think, that circumstances had somehow changed our position. We were no longer nihilist saboteurs; we had become Decadents. As I didn't feel any urge (or talent) to write verse, I could only think of one course that was open to me. I announced that I was going to become a literary critic, though I don't think I then knew exactly what it was literary critics did.

'Hmm,' said Holly to the entire class. 'Yes. I expect Levy here will be a writer.'

Holly, I think, became a Doctor of Divinity and was ordained a minister, though I do not know of what sect. When I last heard of him he was headmaster of a good private school in Lexington. Norma went to her nursing course at the University of Michigan at Ann Arbor, where she managed to add courses in Shakespeare and other things literary to what was then a very il-liberal programme. She was so successful in skirting or re-writing the requirements for becoming a nurse that she managed to get an education, and was eligible to do academic post-graduate work. At first, though, Norma did not exactly pursue her career with great industry. Instead she married a rich northern California doctor, and dedicated herself to becoming a great beauty. When, as it was bound to, the time came to divorce her husband, she abandoned their vast house, with its closets full of the couture clothes he bought her every year at the Paris shows. With only the clothes on her back, she walked into a travel agency and bought a ticket to Tahiti, where she had an affair with a beach boy.

Chapter Ten

My last summer holidays were a bore. Murph was now a tycoon. He owned a pair of stores, originally called Welgo Traders, which cunningly conjured up western Wells Fargo-type images that were very convenient for his advertising. The yokels who came in their thousands, and who were the mainstay of the business, would never have guessed that the attractive name was a composite made up of letters of the Jewish surnames of the three partners. It was a good joke, incorporating the WE of Weil, the L of Levy and, best of all the GO of Goldberg. The concept of the business was Murph's, and it was clever, too. The stores were located in the suburbs where there was plenty of parking, they were open long hours so working people could shop, and the merchandise was arranged so the customers could help themselves, with sales assistants lurking in the background if needed. The aisles were wide enough to permit the passage of supermarket trolleys, which were provided, and you paid for your men's, ladies' and children's clothing, shoes, or general household goods, which included most sorts of soft furnishings, at supermarket checkout stations. It was quick and painless shopping; careful buying, much of which Murph did himself on his frequent trips to New York, meant that there were always bargains to be had.

The sole perk of Murph's new enterprise, so far as I was concerned, was that I was often allowed to accompany him to

New York. This couldn't have been altogether convenient for him, as there were signs and signals, detectable by my prematurely cynical eyes and ears, that Murph led the social life of a bachelor in New York. The greatest bonus of our trips to New York was that we lived in hotels (usually one of Mr Statler's or Mr Hilton's commercial dumps in the garment district, where Murph's buying office was) and were forced to eat in restaurants. Murph considered himself an authority on Manhattan's restaurants. We had Manhattan, tomato-based clam chowder, steamer clams dipped first in clam broth to rid them of their sand, then in melted butter and eaten with the fingers, raw cherrystone clams, bluepoint oysters, Maine lobsters and local bluefish at King of the Sea. We had lasagne at the then gastronomically respectable Mama Leone's: a layer of Bolognese sauce, then one of pasta, followed by layers of ricotta cheese, pasta, sauce, and so on, until it was three inches thick, and topped with a layer of melted mozzarella, browned with parmesan on top. We could have had brilliant Cantonese food at most of the Chinese restaurants we visited, if only we'd known how to order. It was our misfortune that frequenting Wing's Tea House, Lexington's sole essay in the Chinese genre, simply hadn't prepared us for having culinary dealings with genuine and ambitious Chinese restaurants.

Steakhouses were all over the place. Though we had a favourite one, I can't remember its name – or any of the others. What distinguished them from one another? They all served the best quality beef steak available, usually in that cut called 'strip' in New York, and 'New York strip sirloin' in the rest of the world. It was always graded US Prime, which signifies delicious internal marbling of fat, finely veined through the meat, and carrying enough additional cholesterol to bring forward a middle-aged man's first coronary by a month. For the portions were gargantuan. One and one-half inches was the *minimum* thickness of a steak served in any self-respecting New York restaurant, and no menu offered a strip steak weighing less than half a pound. Eighteen ounce monsters were quite common, and twenty not unheard of. The meat was always properly aged and tender, cooked rare to our taste on a charcoal grill, and served with potatoes. Fashions in this article changed in the course of my visits to New York steakhouses (and the rest of the country quickly followed suit) from deep-fried chips or skinny shoestring potatoes, to potatoes baked in their jackets (more accurately, because of their wrappings of aluminium foil, steamed in their jackets) served with soured cream and chives. Meant to be less fattening than chips, the soured cream topping seemed quite delicate in pre-cholesterol days. It was not then usual to drink with food, certainly not wine – but Murph never even had beer. He was more likely to have started his meal with a couple of Scotches on the rocks (in New York, the popular brand was J & B – did Justerini & Brooks know that the natives called it 'Jewish booze'?) or, if he was in a devilish mood, a pair of dry Martinis, an ample quantity, he believed, to make any human being seriously squiffy.

But there were three restaurants where the drink was significant. First, there was a kosher restaurant on the Lower East side, reached by walking up a flight of stairs to the first floor of what appeared to my eyes to be a tenement building. It was called Mama Dubinet's, pronounced as though it were French. Maybe she was French, but the food was certainly not: it was refined *haimische* Jewish food, such as Murph would have got at home if his mother had been a good cook. There, for the first time, I saw the possibilities of *gefilte* fish, poached in excellent fish stock, flavoured with onion, parsley and ground almonds, and served with reasonably fresh horse-radish. The drink? On each table was a syphon of seltzer, soda water; it was instantly replenished by the attentive, wise-cracking, Yiddish-accented waiter, when he heard the whoosh of the last of the bottle. Even those who produced and ate this food every day believed it to be indigestible unless washed down with enough carbon dioxide in solution to make an elephant belch.

Teddy's was so far downtown that it was difficult to get to in the pre-SoHo era. In his restaurant there, the owner Sol Cucinata had invented a proto-nouvelle cuisine, by combining elements of French and Italian dishes, with a then unusual attention to presentation. Sol, being Italian, always chose a bottle of wine for us after he had taken our order. It was a gift from him, as he was a friend of Murph's. (It occurs to me to wonder: 'Sol' is not an Italian name. Could he have been one of the legion of unlikely Jews unearthed by Yiddish-speaking Murph? Once, while we were waiting at a Rome bus stop for a bus to take us to the Vatican, a souvenir seller exhausted his patience and ours by offering us transparencies of St Peter's, holy relics and filthy postcards, all in broken English. Then, pointedly, to blond, blue-eyed Murph, in Yiddish: 'Would you like to go to *shul* with me on Friday night?')

Our family restaurant in New York, though, was Le Veau d'Or. The first time Murph took me there I could not have been more than nine or ten. We were greeted fulsomely, and Murph embraced, by the maître d'hôtel. I had been to a French restaurant before – to a *good* French restaurant, the Maisonette in Cincinnati – and knew what to expect. Even so, I was surprised by the bucket of mussels that was brought to the table, unordered, almost immediately after we sat down. They were in egg yolk-thickened *sauce poulette*, and Murph showed me how to break off one of the halves of the opened mussel shell and use it to scoop out the creamy orange flesh resting on the remaining half shell. You popped it into your mouth and used your crusty bread to mop up your plate and fingers. And you washed it down with white wine – in my case, water tinctured with white wine. It was divine. But I don't remember the rest of the meal, for shortly after the *moules* were cleared away, there was a clatter of falling trays and smashing crockery, and the maître d'hôtel came running through the kitchen swing doors, pursued by the white-hatted chef, armed with his nasty, sharp 8-inch cook's knife. To my astonishment, Murph leapt up from the table and into the fray. He broke up the fight, placed the knife on the table (where I had a long, fascinated look at it), and enjoined the two men to shake hands and make up. Which they did, with the chef returning to the kitchen and the service to normal.

I was too shocked to ask questions; so Murph explained. He hadn't been particularly brave. This had happened before, and he knew he was in no danger. Both the headwaiter and his chef-assailant had worked at the same defence plant as Murph during the war; one of them was always getting up the other's nose, but they were always easily disarmed, both physically and emotionally, by any bystander. Oh. We finished our meal without interruption.

It is, strictly speaking, outside the time boundaries of this narrative, but I should like to memorialise my last meal at Le Veau d'Or. I was alone in New York, probably waiting to catch the next day's 'daylight' flight to London, and I telephoned Murph for advice on where to have dinner. He suggested Le Veau d'Or (which must surely have changed hands once or twice since the 1950s) for 'auld lang syne'. I telephoned to book a table, was greeted in French and, linguistically wrong-footed, reserved my table in the same language without even thinking about it.

I was met at the door, this time by a woman, greeted, again in French, and asked if I'd like to go directly to what was, *malheureusement*, not the best table. (The restaurant was shaped like a railway carriage, with banquettes lining either wall.) I volunteered to sit at the bar and nurse a *pastis* until a better table came free. Finally, I was ushered to a table less than two feet away from a couple whose history was instantly deducible from their appearances and overheard conversation. He was a middle-aged Jewish doctor, with a successful practice in New Rochelle. He was divorced from the mother of his dining-companion, his extremely plain daughter, a university student whose recent and first love affair had just gone very wrong. Though the reason never became clear to me, she blamed her father for this. They were not enjoying their meal.

The waiter continued to speak French to me, and offered me a dish or two not on the menu. I began with oysters, I think and then accepted the waiter's suggestion of *boudin noir* with apples, which was presumably not on the menu because Americans might have been squeamish about blood pudding. When my main course arrived, father and daughter, badly in need of distraction from their own woes, asked each other 'What's that?' and why there wasn't anything of its description on the English menu. 'I suppose,' hypothesised the daughter, 'that they give special treatment here to other French people.' She had made the elementary, but understandable error, of thinking that, because I spoke French, I didn't know English.

They carried on in the same manner, obviously relieved that I couldn't have followed their own painful conversation, and grateful that my presence had provided them with a change of topic. 'What's he doing here on his own?' demanded the doctor. 'Where's his wife tonight?' 'Can't you tell he's *queer*?' replied the jilted daughter getting her own back on at least one male. 'Yes, you must be right,' said the father, entering into the spirit of the game, 'he's had an argument with his boyfriend, and that's why he's out all alone.' They went on, too, agreeing that it was just like the French to seek solace for a broken heart in food and wine, and that I was drinking too much – both white *and* red wine, and that wasn't it odd that the French care so much about their food that they don't even mind eating it alone. They speculated on what I did, judging from my clothes that I was definitely not in business, but not flashy enough to be a hairdresser, interior decorator or in the theatre; they concluded that my boyfriend must be in one of the above typical professions, and that it must be he who was keeping me on the proceeds of it.

166

As I have seldom been better entertained at dinner, I found it quite easy to resist the temptation to wish them 'good evening' when I got up from the table. I left the restaurant without having uttered a single word of English.

One more New York meal with Murph has to be recorded. It too is out of sequence – and bounds – here, but for me was an historic occasion. I was at Harvard. Murph and I were not getting on; as usual, the dispute was over money. In fact, I was very near being financially independent of him, which probably made things worse. He telephoned me from New York, and said that if I'd agree to see him, just for the evening, he'd take me to Le Pavillon on East 57th Street. Le Pavillon was the best restaurant in America, and this must have been the last year or the last but one of the life of its owner, the great Henri Soulé, after whose death in 1966 the restaurant just went to pieces. It occurs to me now (though it didn't occur to me then) to wonder how Murph managed to make a reservation for dinner there on a few hours' notice, for Soulé practically invented New York restaurant snobbery by making it difficult for any but his favoured regular customers to get a table.

I took the shuttle to La Guardia, and arrived at Murph's hotel in time for a drink before dinner. I can recall every mouthful of that meal. It began with champagne, which we continued to drink with the *billi-bi*, cold, strongly saffron-flavoured mussel stock, enriched and made silky with cream. Fillet of beef *à la financière* was correctly garnished with truffles, cocks' combs and kidneys – think how many fowl were required to give up their tiny kidneys to provide what was on each of our plates. With it we drank an ancient Chambertin, '52 I should think. The *tarte aux framboises* was served with each perfect berry facing the right way, pointed end outwards. When I got back after midnight to my house on Harvard Street in Cambridge, Mass., I found that my flat-mate was just serving eight or ten guests the last course of an enormous Chinese meal he'd cooked to console himself for missing Henri Soulé's. So I finished the night with soup cooked in an entire scooped-out and steamed watermelon.

Murph could be curiously and unexpectedly generous. When we were in New York he would often allow me certain expensive metropolitan juvenile indulgences. For example, I was almost always taken to see the latest Broadway musical, and sometimes even to something more serious, such as Richard Burton's *Hamlet*. Tickets for these came, I presume, from his business connections, for we could never have got them ourselves with less than six months' planning ahead.

One evening, though, he astonished me by suggesting that I take two Lexington girls to a nightclub. Perhaps I had already reached eighteen, the legal drinking age in New York, so at least his scheme wasn't positively against the law. It was definitely out of character, though, for Murph, who was always trying to instil a bit of puritanical restraint into my hedonistic impulsiveness, to initiate – and pay for – my premature initiation into these particular pleasures of the flesh. Flesh there was. The sight of the heaving bare tits and long, long legs of Manhattan's classiest and flashiest showgirls at (I think I remember) the Copacabana was shared with Joanne and Gail Wides. They were probably in New York with Murph's great friend, their uncle, 'Cokey' Hymson. Gail was a couple of years older than me; Joanne a few days younger. I was a little frightened of the stern manner of Gail (who became an academic mathematician); but Joanne I remember most for her perpetual larky good humour, and the fact that, when we were very small children, she could use her tiny, pointy front teeth to nibble a hole in the bottom of a chocolate and, if she didn't like the centre, replace it in the Whitman's Sampler box without anyone being able to tell that it had been previously sampled. The Wides girls had lived down the road from us on Cooper Drive, and both made great and important contributions to my sex education. They were the first females who ever shared my bed: I had got rubella,

German measles. In those days there was no immunising injection against it, and the Wides girls each spent a night in turn with me in the hopes of catching the disease. They were also the first girls I ever saw naked on purpose. (I think I had seen one or two in that state – but not under conditions I could reveal to my parents.) I remember being taken to spend the night at their house and the three of us being bathed together. I remember nothing at all of my feelings on first officially encountering the female genitalia. What I remember is that their mother, Evelyn, allowed them to eat apples in the bath.

Murph gave me $100 (in cash, of course; these were pre-credit-card days, in any case). He had told me to tip the 'Maître d', which I did, and we were duly given a table that actually touched the stage. Of course, when the show started, we realised that this was not at all a desirable place to be. It was so close to the action that, even craning your neck, all you could do was look up the girls' legs. We saw plenty of G-strings and cache-sexes that night, but no faces. Murph had actually told me to give the girls dinner, and said we could have a drink apiece. Provided we didn't order champagne, the money he had given me would cover the entire bill, plus tips and taxis. I don't think I was embarrassed by the show or by our pretending to be more grown-up than we were. But what on earth was Murph's motive for sending us to a nightclub on our own? He and his friend were both unmarried and on the loose at that time. I suppose they had mounted their own evening's entertainment, and required us to be out of the way.

By the time of my last two years at school, Murph had already bought out his partners, and the businesses had grown huge. One of the shops, for example, was located in the former premises of a vast supermarket; and that was the smaller of the two stores. At one point (though I think his partners still retained an interest in the buildings themselves), Murph owned an entire city block, including his own store, its warehouse, a large drugstore, an ice cream parlour and premises that alternated between being a sleazy nightclub and the local social security offices. We even had our own bank, as it were; an enterprising local bank had built a branch office exactly next door for the purpose of receiving the daily cash takings from Murph's business.

I loathed it. Murph made me work a large part of each summer, for a small wage, stacking shirts according to their style, price, collar size and sleeve size, and endlessly taking inventories of stocks of work trousers, Y-fronts, socks and winter coats, all evil-smelling, though I cannot imagine why they should have been so. Though he pretended I was there to learn the business from the ground floor up, I never graduated to the next storey. Literally speaking, there wasn't one: the stores were one-floor.

My father knew perfectly well that as soon as I went to college, wherever that might be, I wasn't coming back to Lexington. I had been one of the finalists in the first years of the national Merit Scholarships programme, and there were many other signs to read that said that I was going to have an academic career. In truth, that was what he wanted for me. Had circumstances and history been different, he might have done the same himself. The summer job was a penance – but for what? For my short-lived attempt to be a juvenile delinquent? For what must have looked to him like my defection to my mother and step-father? Or was the summer job perhaps just an excuse to keep me physically closer to himself, by imprisoning me for eight hours a day in *his* building?

The work was spirit-breaking, the pay was bad, the conditions unpleasant. I had always to be near the selling-floor, tape measure always at the ready to enlighten a smelly farm-worker as to the length of his inside leg, and then to retrieve and refold the unwanted garments from the curtained booth where, partly undressed to try them on, he revealed his great need for Lifebuoy soap.

During the lunch break I escaped to next-door DeJarnette drugstore (unaware then that Murph was the landlord) to munch my olive-nut or pimiento-cheese-on-toast sandwich, washed down by iced tea, unsweetened but flavoured with lemon juice, while sitting at the soda fountain reading *I, Claudius* or *Far from the Madding Crowd*. Murph had asked me not to sit around and read in the staff lounge during the lunch break, as it set a bad example.

In my very last year I escaped for a few weeks to the University of Kentucky, where I began my ambivalent relationship with the German language. I was good at it, as good as any of the post-graduate students who were cramming to take their language requirement exams, and almost as good as my friend Bob Miller. A few years older than I, he was either an undergraduate at Haverford or just preparing to take up his Rhodes scholarship at St Antony's College, Oxford. At the end of those few weeks I could both read and speak a little German, and remained able to do so until the mid-sixties, when a Cologne bus ran into my car. (I was driver and interpreter for my girlfriend and another couple, but when I got out of my car to expostulate with the bus driver, I could not remember a syllable of his language. Later that day, at the unhelpful American consulate at Bad Gödesburg, I swooned and fell onto the terrazzo floor. I had 'flu. We were repatriated by the British consulate, whose behaviour was in sharp and edifying contrast to that of the consulate of the country whose passport I held.) As a post-graduate student at Harvard I was required to take stiff examinations in German, French and Latin as well as Anglo-Saxon. I had to learn German all over again, and had only a dim memory of its conjugations and especially declensions. I sailed through the philosophy department's exam, did badly in the English department's exam, and got almost perfect marks in the national exam. I immediately forgot the language wholesale once more. Then, in 1980 I was sent to Frankfurt by the *New York Times*, and realised one drunken night that I was having a conversation with my taxi driver, and we weren't speaking English.

This last summer, I went, as I had done the two summers before, to yet another camp in Ohio. I don't remember its name; but I remember its purpose: it was a continuation of Cotillion by other means. Or rather, it was a combination marriage broker- age and school for political activists. It was the leadership training institute of the Ohio Valley Federation of Temple Youth, and I shall try to write this chapter without resorting to any of the cute acronyms we used to refer to it.

The Reform, i.e. liberal, branch of American Judaism trained its rabbinical students at Cincinnati, at Hebrew Union College. In the era of which I am writing, just post-McCarthy and pre- Martin Luther King, they (and a lot of other theological semi- naries) were in the position of the mediaeval monasteries which preserved Western culture from the Barbarians. As clergy, and would-be clergy, they were immune from investigation by McCarthy and the unfunny clowns of the House Un-American Activities Committee, and able to convince themselves that it was their religious duty to be the repository of lay liberal values.

The Temple Youth Movement, the youth arm of Reform Jewry (as opposed to the individually smaller, but more numer- ous Orthodox, Conservative and Zionist youth groups) took its lead from the Cincinnati seminary. We in the Ohio Valley, being on its doorstep, got our orders direct. While it might seem unfair to lump us Lexington youth in with youth from Ohio, West Virginia and Indiana when we (and the kids from Louisville) were separated from them by the audible social gulf of our drawls, geography ruled, and we did not meet the eligible Jewish girls of Cleveland, Chicago, Atlanta or Boston. (Bob Miller did, though, as he was the President of the national organisation.)

For that was what it was – mostly – about, from the punter's point of view. This was not, of course, the outlook of the red brigade of rabbis.

We were only lightly supervised at camp. Our elected leaders – such as me – were expected to do this for the younger and those with lesser leadership ability. So we always did our rounds and checked that the boys and girls, who ranged in age from about fourteen to eighteen, were tucked up in their beds, with their cabin lights off, before we got down to the evening's business. This never varied: it was how to arrange to get laid.

So long as the sun shone, we were there to pursue peace, racial harmony and social justice; the pursuit of sex was strictly after-hours. We wrote and performed psycho-dramas about what you would do if you were turned away from a lunch counter or a cinema because one of your companions was black. We held workshops on how to deal with the bigotry of people in authority, such as teachers. We exchanged views on how to organise protests – this was before the Civil Rights movement started. We debated the demerits of the atomic bomb.

We held what were supposed to be daily religious services, but in place of the unintelligible Hebrew hymns of my youth we sang: 'Hiroshima, Nagasaki,/ Lord, beyond the blue,/ Alamogordo, Bikini:/ It could happen to you!' On the duplicating machine we printed the words to all the important songs; rightly, I think, we reckoned knowing them the most important of all leadership skills. Mostly they were Pete Seeger songs, or those sung by his group, the Weavers.

'If I had a hammer, I'd hammer out Freedom.' '*Die Gedenken sind frei*, my thoughts freely flower. *Die Gedenken sind frei*, my thoughts give me power.' 'This land is my land, this land is your land.' 'Oh, the banks are made of marble, with a guard at every door, and the vaults are stuffed with silver, that the PEOPLE sweated for.' Sometimes, around the campfire or after the execrable meals served in the communal dining room, there was singing of songs with less ferocious words, simple murder ballads such as, 'So only say that you'll be mine,/ and in no other arms entwine,/ down beside where the waters flow,/ down by the banks of the Ohio,' appropriately enough. And even sweetly messageless folk songs like 'The fox went out on a moon-lit night' and the odd nonsense song. But our taste definitely lay in the direction of the political lyric, and we liked the big themes: Liberty, Justice and Nuclear Annihilation. We were good kids, just sentimental.

One or two of Norma's and my fellow school espionage specialists followed us to camp. Were we hypocrites? Even cynical manipulators of our peers? I don't think so. In the first place, religion had nothing to do with our presence there. The hip young rabbis had long ago, if perversely, disposed of this point, by arguing that the struggle for social justice is the first imperative of religion. They were sincere; but if the times had been different they would have been out on picket lines, instead of in their seminaries. A few years later this is just what did happen. As for us, we were fundamentally irreligious, and happy to accept any argument that allowed us to enjoy ourselves and sing such fine songs, in praise and in support of things we really could believe in – unlike poor old God.

We knew what we were at summer camp for, and so did our parents. We were there to enlarge the ghettos. In Lexington there were maybe a dozen Jewish girls my age or a little younger, who could have been considered eligible marriage partners for me. Although I never even succeeded in going to bed with any of them while we were still living in Lexington (not for want of trying, however), and though we were all certain when we left Lexington to go to our universities (which almost every one of us did) to meet some more eligible mates, the amateur anthropologist that possesses part of the soul of every Jewish mother knew instinctively that it could only be a good thing to enlarge the pool of those eligible to marry their children. Even the most emancipated of Lexington Jewish mothers, Shirley for instance, would admit to having a marginal preference that her sons should marry nice Jewish girls.

Here, at Camp Nookie, there were nothing but nice Jewish girls. The problem was: how, when and where to do it? In this goal, many of the girls were fully complicit. The girls had to be 'leaders' – part of the power structure, just as we boys were – to be out of our bunks after lights out. But there were adequate numbers of leaders of each sex to allow pairing off. The trouble was there was nowhere to go except the infirmary, whose beds were fully occupied by sick kids or the nurse; the bedroom belonging to the director and his wife, who were not sleeping in it themselves, but could hear from it mischief emanating from most quarters, including the deserted dining hall. So long as the sounds that came from there were of at least four of us playing bridge, there was no curfew or attempt at discipline. If the numbers sounded as though they were fewer or engaged in less formal pastimes, the director would invariably wake from his light slumbers. That left Nature – the great outdoors, the wilderness. We tried it, but we didn't like it.

Even with a clandestinely transported blanket thrown over the stubby grass and weeds, Nature was not user-friendly. Dogs would bark, sounding too close. Were they attached to owners? Wasn't it worse if they weren't? Mosquito repellent cannot have been invented then; at least we never had any. Ouch, a nasty pointy weed has just pierced the blanket and your lady's naked thigh and drawn blood. It never even got to the have-you-remembered-to-bring-the-rubbers?-stage of tenderness. An insect bite or a rustling in the grass that was all too likely to be a snake generally resulted in the conclusion that Old Adam could never have had to cope with this vicious, non-Edenic Nature; and back to camp one stole with the still-virgin Eve.

Once in a while, the routine changed, and we were quick to take advantage. The population of campers turned over completely every ten or fourteen days, and sometimes there was a camper-less interlude, with one lot leaving, say, Sunday afternoon and the next not arriving until Monday morning.

A girl I'll call Dinah and I had been dallying for some time; we seized the day – or rather the early evening, for the director and his wife were going out to a local eatery. Well before sunset Dinah and I were esconced in my own bed, in a semi-private room sandwiched between two twelve-bed cabins, from which I was meant to exert moral authority over the boys who slept on either side. Dinah was not exactly plain – her face had 'character'. Her hair was dark, black, really, and curled tightly, so tightly you'd have to call it kinky. On her oval face, her luxuriant eyebrows surmounted always animated dark brown eyes. Her nose was small, but not mean, and her mouth generous. Her upper lip showed the beginnings of fine, black down.

Although I liked Dinah, I wasn't passionate about her. Still, she had a keen sense of humour; we laughed a lot. And she was as eager as I was. Moreover, under her blouse were two firm and interesting breasts, and her shorts revealed long shapely legs, terminating in ample, rounded hips and buttocks. Dinah had a good body. I didn't forget the courtship. It seemed like hours had passed, and Dinah was still dressed in her bra and knickers. The latter came off first. It seemed more nonchalant to do it in that order. Feeling suave and sophisticated, I somewhat later turned my attention to undoing and removing the bra. Child's play. Off came my Y-fronts. It had taken a long time and much planning to achieve this situation.

By the glow of the fading light I could see that Dinah was excited, perhaps as excited as I. Was the packet of condoms under the pillow? It was. Nuzzling Dinah's breasts with my face, my eyes shut, I could feel her erect nipple, firm and standing proud of the areola, itself stretched taut. And I could feel something else, too. A hair. I opened my eyes. It was a hair, a single glossy blue-black hair, growing immediately under the darker brown circle of skin at the centre of Dinah's breast. There was one on the other breast, too.

I tried very hard not to laugh.

Would the hairs on Dinah's chest affect my ardour? Perhaps they would further excite me. Who knows? I think Dinah had already had an orgasm, which was just as well, for as I was pondering her hirsute tits our bridge partners crashed into my bedroom. They found our posture hilarious. Nancy, the wit, pronounced it a case of 'coitus interruptus' to her own complete satisfaction. She and Archie, our usual fourth, began to guffaw uncontrollably, and collapsed on the other twin bed, staring at us between bouts of breathless mirth. We were too stunned to cover ourselves up. Did they notice the hairs?

Dinah and I had another go, in a tacky hotel in some city where youth group business took us. I cannot recall what happened this time to interfere with the mutual loss of virginity; but something went wrong – or half wrong. We were both sexually satisfied, but agreed that it didn't really count as 'going all the way'. The hairs were still there.

It makes one feel like Frank Harris, broken and broke in Nice, cooking up *My Life and Loves* to pay the bills, but all I can bring back to mind from those summers are the girls. I remember Karen from West Virginia, with a confident mouth and frank eyes, long legs and a good seat on a horse; Anna, whose copper-coloured hair was echoed by the triangle of her mound of Venus; tall, leggy Juliet, with dead straight, silky pubic hair; and the little girl, whose name I have forgotten, who was beautiful and vulnerable and sang 'Moonlight in Vermont' in a husky, sexy contralto, so perfectly that I believed her when she said she sang professionally, with a band. But the song that so enchanted me was the whole of her repertory; she couldn't manage a note of any other song.

And there was Nancy, the wit. (I'm using her real name, to get even with her for the scene with Dinah.) We found exactly the same things laughable which of course led some people to conclude that we were sick or mad. We often suffered from a form of *folie à deux*, in which something would strike us as funny – a girl wearing a completely hideous dress of which she was obviously inordinately fond, or the too-practised grin of an obsequious young man – and we'd laugh until the tears ran, though nobody else present could even see that there *was* a joke.

Nancy was a little older, and had started university a year before me. She was going to be in Cincinnati one day, when Lil was going to see her accountant and had invited me to dine with her at the Maisonette. I persuaded her to invite Nancy too.

The Maisonette has, for as long as I can remember, been one of the best restaurants in America. It is not all that remarkable that it should be located in Cincinnati, for there have been periods when Cincinnati was able to support two serious French restaurants. Lil made a habit of taking me to the Maisonette when she had business in Cincinnati, because I had behaved, by her lights, so very well the first time, when I was eight or nine. Recently back from France, and learning French herself from a private teacher (she had weekly conversation lessons with a local French lady, which always led me to suspect that she had someone special to talk to back in Paris), Lil translated the menu for me. *Quiche Lorraine?* Bacon tart. Never had it, sounds interesting. *Boeuf en daube?* Just beef stew, by the sound of it. *Coq au vin?* Lillian makes that at home. *Foie de veau?* Even Shirley can cook calf's liver. So I settled on the one thing I'd never had, couldn't imagine, and which Lola couldn't translate, and I ordered the tripe. Fortunately, I liked it. In fact, I loved it, and didn't leave a morsel of it in the serving bowl, *and* swabbed my plate clean of sauce with a hunk of baguette. I was a gastronomic hit. The waiters loved it. Lola swanked all the way back to the car.

Now, many *choucroutes, cassoulets, boeufs modes, sautés de veau, pâtés, terrines* and hundreds of *escargots* later, there are dark-haired, winsomely freckle-faced Nancy and I, seated across from each other on the banquettes in the scene of my childhood's gastronomic triumphs, embarrassing Lil by looking likerishly at each other over the *pot au feu*. A slurp of the *bouillion* and a tongue passed meaningfully over the lips. Lil couldn't miss it. Over the *tarte aux pommes*, Nancy announced that she was coming to Lexington with us.

Lil must have thought it was the Beaujolais. Well brought-up girls didn't – propose themselves. This one did, though, and she wasn't going to be budged. 'But where will she stay, dear? Such short notice and all?' 'Oh, she'll stay with me at Shirley's,' said I, saying exactly the wrong thing. 'In the guest room.' 'Well, dear, perhaps you should telephone your mother and give her a little warning.' 'Oh no, she won't expect it. I often bring friends home,' I fibbed, concealing with my napkin the 18-year-old's erection that would be revealed if I stood up to use the phone.

Lil did *her* best to conceal her own crossness. I was made to sit at the back of the car for the two-hour drive back home. I was glad. It gave me time to fantasise about exactly what I was going to do to Nancy, and she to me.

By the time we arrived at Indian Mound Road, Lil was in a southern well-I-never mood. Shirley made it much worse by deciding to score off her sister, and being blasé rather than outraged by my behaviour. We had already thanked Lil for the dinner and the lift. Now Shirley ostentatiously said she was tired, and bade good night to Lil. To Nancy and me she said, in a way that clearly (but falsely) implied that this happened all the time: 'Make sure you're in separate rooms when the maid comes in tomorrow morning. Night night.'

Nancy and I were, of course, hysterical. We collapsed in shrieks. That's not all that collapsed. I don't know what the state of Nancy's virginity was at the beginning of the evening, but my own was the same at the end. We laughed about that, too.

Chapter Eleven

One thing I always hated about Lexington was the University of Kentucky football and basketball games. Tickets for them changed hands at a premium, but through the good offices of one of their buddies, Babe and Uncle Louis, who had no alumnus connections, got several good and valuable season tickets year after year, as did Murph, who, as a graduate, was entitled to them in his own right. This was a misery for me, because everybody insisted that I *must* enjoy the privilege of what amounted to having a permanent seat of my own for every home football and basketball match.

In the first place, I was bored. I could not see the point of enduring the discomfort of cold autumn days to sit outside on a hard folding seat and watch a lot of grown – no, overgrown – boys wearing stupid costumes more suited to a war than to a game, move an obloid leather ball across a field divided into ten-yard portions. As for basketball: though it was played indoors, in more comfort, I could not see the point of America having bred a race of seven-foot giants whose only task was to tip a sphere into a net. On the whole, I thought the British were right to treat it as a game for girls.

My dislike of these expensive gladiatorial events was well-known. I was forced to come along with the rest of the family, every single member of whom had tickets, either to cure me of my cissy feelings about games, or for the more probable reason that it was difficult and cost more than the price of the ticket to hire a babysitter for me.

Perversely, there was one bit of these afternoons and evenings that I enjoyed. If you got there exactly at the beginning, you would be in time for the singing, over the public address system and accompanied by the UK Marching band, of the national anthem. This was always followed by a hush, and then the crowd singing, choking back the tears, the sentimental Stephen Collins Foster song: 'Oh the sun shines bright/ on my old Kentucky home,/ 'Tis summer, the darkies are gay'. There was no Civil Rights, Gay Lib nonsense in those far-away days: black men were 'darkies' and so long as they had their watermelon quota, gay, too. It went on, through its high-pitched chorus with mounting hysteria to its heart-wrenching climax: 'Weep no more, my lady, / [then, *piano*] O, weep no more today. / We will sing one song / for the old Kentucky home, / for the old Kentucky home / far away . . . By and by hard times / come a-knockin' at the door. / Then my old Kentucky home, good night.'

I derived unfailing pleasure from the behaviour of the crowd on these occasions. There was at this point not a dry eye amongst the tens of thousands present (some lubricated by pint bottles of Bourbon being nipped at clandestinely from their concealing brown paper bags). Yet the all-white crowd made up of rednecks, crackers, yokels, recently rich hillbillies, less recently impoverished southern aristocrats, and respectable Jewish doctors, lawyers and businessmen would always, in a fraction of a second, compose themselves, and with triumphant bathos, in a shout whose volume would have undone the foundations of Jericho, exhort the home team, telling them tersely what to do with the rival visiting side: 'KILL 'EM!'

Now the time had come – at last – for me, with defiantly dry eye, to leave my old Kentucky home. I had been looking forward to it for some time. The only question had to do, not with the manner of my leaving, but with my destination. I had no college to go to, thanks to my unloved and troublesome first name.

The bureaucracy of the American university system is one of the great jokes of the universe. Only someone with a masochistic streak and an insatiable appetite for practical jokes could have devised it. It was, and remains, easier to master the British welfare rules for eligibility for supplementary benefit rates rebates than to fathom how to apply for admission as an undergraduate to an American university.

For one thing, as you'll have noticed if you've ever filled in a US visa application form, all the peoples of the earth are meant to be christened something that can be written as 'Last name . . . First name . . . Middle initial.' I was gored on the horns of a dilemma. To comply with this demand for a standardised name meant that the resulting appellation would not match the one on my school records. These records had followed me all the way through the Fayette County School system, since I was recruited into it at the age of six, and my mother, not I, had suppressed my first name. At school I was 'Paul', *simpliciter*.

To solve this problem we consulted the best minds of Lafayette High School. They recommended using the first initial and middle name, on the application forms to Harvard, Yale, Princeton and Haverford, a splendid, small Quaker four-year liberal arts college near Philadelphia. Golden boy Bob Miller had got his first degree there, and easily persuaded me to add it in case I experienced a change of mind about the Ivy League giants.

In any case I was going to Harvard, and the whole nerve-wracking business was redundant. I was going to graduate with very good marks, though not so perfect as to make the professional admissions officers employed to do this thankless job think I was a grind, wimp or nerd. I had as good references as ever came from Lafayette. (The principal, though he was looking forward to seeing the back of me, was desperate to unload me on Harvard.) I had, in only the fourth year of a national competitive examination, become a Merit Scholar, though oxymoronically was not actually given a scholarship because though I merited it, my family did not have financial need of it.

Still, this resulted in offers of places – and financial assistance and even financial incentives to accept – from a dozen universities I'd never heard of, and one I had: Tulane, in New Orleans. I'd done very well indeed in the College Board exams. In the morning 'scholastic aptitude tests' I'd got a high score for maths and 799 out of 800 for English; in the afternoon special subject exams, my abysmal Latin score was balanced by my stunning chemistry score and perfect marks for English.

There was every reason for me to be cocky. But I listened to Abe Wikler, anyway, and applied to the private, Rockefeller-founded, eccentric, Bolshevik-minded University of Chicago, just to satisfy Abe's whim.

Murph had already taken me to Meyers and bought me an entire new wardrobe to kit me out for life in the Ivy League. As I was going to be a Harvard man, my not always open-handed father even ordered a bespoke suit and jacket for me, the first clothes that were ever made for me.

Computers had not yet been employed to take the drudgery out of the admissions process, and every application was handled individually by people employed to do it. Since, like me, most aspirants made multiple applications – there was no limit except that of your own purse for the fees – it was a hell of a job, and not normally finished until mid-June or even later.

So it was well into summer when we heard I had not got a university place. Murph kick-started himself into action. We were on a plane for Boston before you could say John Quincy Adams. And it only took a little persistence to get the admissions officer to admit that the trouble was an 'incomplete application': no College Board scores.

Why hadn't they written to advise us of this earlier? Well, there *were* 11.2 million applications for every single place in next year's freshman class, and it was difficult to look at any individual application until the time of final judgement. Yes, the hapless bureaucrat agreed (these jobs were generally done by university groupies, who were not qualified to teach – or, for that matter, to do anything else at all), the missing exam results were quite easy to find. In the folder next to the one from which they were absent, in fact.

But no, there was no possibility of rectifying the mistake this coming autumn. To allow for multiple applications, Harvard always admitted five per cent (or so) more freshmen than there were places for; but this year, most of them had taken up the offer, so unless some boys died before the end of September, they were going to have a problem fitting them all into Harvard Yard. A 'transfer' the year after, perhaps.

We looked in at Haverford as well. They found the missing file, instantly assented that there was no reason I should not come to Haverford, except, look for yourselves (and we did) at this lilliputian campus. They could not make room for an additional undergraduate without embarking on a building programme.

From Philadelphia we flew to Chicago. Murph, made miserable at first by the left-wing reputation of the U of C, cheered up a lot when he saw its Gothic campus, many of the buildings copied from Oxford, but with the proportions sometimes comically wrong. Even better was the robust right-wing attitude of the professional admissions officer: why, sir, didn't you know, sir, this is the university of Milton Friedman and Friedrich von Hayek, of Frank Knight, of Enrico Fermi, the father of the atomic bomb, of Amos Alonzo Stagg, the great Big Ten football coach, of Aristotle and St Thomas Aquinas. Conservatism? We invented it.

The missing file was found, the rejection withdrawn on the spot. A telegram of acceptance awaited our arrival home.

Murph remained apprehensive. A couple of years later, the same admissions officer, conservatively dressed in Ivy League clothes, was sitting next to me on a bar stool at Jimmy's, the university bar, buying me double whiskeys with beer chasers and trying to put his hand on my knee.

The blow to my self-esteem was great. It required a new way of thinking about myself, my peers and the world. At first, I was satisfied that it was just bad luck that Murph's (and my own) ambition had been so thwarted. But soon the feeling of having been rejected set in. Mitch Gail was going from Andover to Harvard, Bob Miller was either at Oxford or Harvard Law School, and Mike Ades at Edinburgh or Yale. I'd let the side down, too.

My first days at the University of Chicago were giddy. I lived in a brand new dormitory; from the window of my room you could see Frank Lloyd Wright's Robie House in close-up. I met the other boys on the same floor the first night I was there. There was an enormous contingent of boys (and, I learnt the next day, girls as well), Jews from New York, who thought the world, and more, of themselves. Most of them were from families who had been Communist Party members.

This was top secret: if they hadn't hidden this away with extreme care, my admissions officer's Bolshevik-detector would have assured that they did not get into the University of Chicago – which every single one of them insisted was his first choice. Their parents' former communism made a bond among them that no outsider could share; it gave the girls an air of secrecy so palpable that you might have thought they were all pregnant – and pleased about it. It took only minutes for me to agree with their own estimate of their intrinsic superiority.

Three boys, who already knew each other from New York, descended upon me. They had persecution in mind. Was I sure I was Jewish? The name was in order, but my looks? What had I done with myself in Lexington? Burnt crosses? Beat niggers?

At that point an older boy, the dormitory prefect, broke in and stopped it. He was from Kansas City, I think, but had a touch of a drawl. His name was John Snowday, and at first, I was more frightened of him than of my New York Jewish tormentors. I soon established impeccably liberal credentials – for a southerner – and was invited out for an absolutely illicit beer. These were to be my friends, and something more, for the next several years. Two of them died in their youth, and I still grieve over the waste.

At the time, though, the main thing was the inferiority I felt to them – in intellect and in social, athletic and even sexual prowess. The dotty University of Chicago system didn't help either. It was modelled on Oxford, except that the first thing you did on arrival was to take the equivalent of the Schools examinations, on the plausible grounds that it was a waste of your time to study anything you already know. So you were excused ('placed out') from any of the required subjects you could show you had already mastered.

There were faculty 'advisers' to interpret the results of these exams for the new undergraduates (to set us apart from other, lesser universities, we were never called 'freshmen'). My adviser evidently had a low opinion of southern high school education, and shared my own rapidly descending assessment of my own cleverness, for he never told me the obvious conclusion to be drawn from my performance in these examinations. It was not until the end of my third year, when it was too late to make the arrangements, that I was told I was formally qualified to graduate after just the three years. I had been excused an entire year of my university course.

This has to count as a massive deviation from the true course of my tale, however. There is still Lexington to leave behind. The major social event of one's senior year at school is, of course, the Senior Prom. I do not know what prompted me to ask Pamela Brown to accompany me to my Senior Prom. Or why she accepted – given my reputation, it was a sporting thing to do, like Faust accompanying Mephistopheles to the mountain top. I certainly did not know then that she was to become part-heiress, to the extent of 30 million dollars, I believe, to the Kentucky Fried Chicken fortune. (Her brother, John Y. Brown jnr, was involved in the development of the franchising of Kentucky Fried Chicken. He has recently been Governor of Kentucky, and married Phyllis George, a former Miss America.) I just had a crush on her.

That's why I eschewed the ordinary, normal corsage of gardenias a beau normally bought to pin on his date's formal evening dress, and instead demanded that the harassed florist make a tiara of white carnations. He hadn't a clue what I was talking about, so I drew it for him, badly. Of course, it wouldn't stay up. But Pam tolerantly tied it to her wrist, and gave no sign that she was anything but pleased to have received a floral tribute so eccentric and so different from those given to the other girls.

It must have been the delicacy of puppy love (finely ironic this, from a boy who'd made a career of failing to get laid by half the girls in the Ohio Valley) that made me wish to even up my sideboards. I gashed myself so badly with my safety razor that Shirley had to put a large plaster on my face. ('Tell her you cut yourself shaving,' she said unkindly as I walked out the front door.)

Did I ever see Pam Brown again? Did she fade out of my life after one giddy whirl around the dance floor of youth? I read, years ago, that Pam had married and that the young couple had been lost at sea (were they trying to cross the Atlantic?) in a hot air balloon. Had I pursued my courtship of Pamela Brown, the outcome would have been somewhat different. You can bet that I would not have been in that balloon.

At university I read philosophy. Plato once saved my life. I have already mentioned that someone, out to get Murph, had fiddled my position in the conscription lottery. I got notice that I was to be drafted, just as I was leaving to return to England. I asked for a 'voluntary' medical examination, a procedure you could invoke if you had some reason to think you might be unable to do military service on medical grounds. I was sent for examination to Dr Welcome, whose sons, Tommy and Johnny, had been acquaintances – through Cotillion, I should think; we weren't at school together.

'Well now,' drawled the well-disposed Dr Welcome. 'What's going to keep you out of the army?' I confidently suggested that he look at the surgeon's report on my right femur. (He had all my medical records, except the recent ones I had acquired at university). 'Very interesting,' he said, and looked it up in a sort of army manual of injuries. 'According to this book,' he said, 'either you have no right leg, or you have never had the injuries described in the surgeon's report.' The army had not yet caught up with the surgical techniques that had saved my leg; so far as they were concerned the remedy for my – now alleged – injuries was amputation.

'Now this won't do,' said the doctor, looking at the X-rays and examining my leg. 'They'll break it again on the first day of basic training. But I can't let you off for a condition the army says doesn't exist. Got any chronic conditions?'

I remained nervously silent as he picked his way through my medical file. He looked up from it, and asked: 'What're you studying in London?' I answered, 'Philosophy.' 'Philosophy?' He looked pleased. 'John's majoring in philosophy at' (I think he went on to say) 'Princeton.' Then he reached for his wallet, and extracted a yellowing newspaper cutting from it. It was one of those short columns of inspirational verse small town newspapers used to print every day. This, from the Lexington *Herald* or *Leader*, was about Plato seeing the true God in his Forms. Dr Welcome added another tear to those that had already fallen on this antique newsprint, and solemnly, with deliberation, folded it back up and replaced it in his billfold.

'Now, what've we got wrong with you?' In seconds he unearthed the account of my dealings, four or five years earlier, with Maurie Kaufmann. At that time, Maurie had made a long list of ailments that were typically found in patients who had my acute allergies. He had said the list would one day stand me in good stead. 'Ahah,' Dr Welcome pronounced with unaffected satisfaction, 'a history of bronchial asthma. That'll do nicely.' Hypochondria pays.

That's how I went to London, where I never meant to stay. That was the real end of my childhood. It was the end, too, for the boys unlucky enough to be drafted the next day. Following their basic training in the 101st Airborne Division at Fort Campbell, Kentucky, they went to Vietnam. I don't expect many of them returned.

The sound of the milkman leaving a couple of pints in our wooden letterbox on a wintry Saturday morning set off a whole train of reflections. I have never stopped to think why I have ended up in middle age, living in a seventeenth-century farm-house, with a muddy farmyard in front of me and a barn full of dairy cows behind me. I made no conscious choices about where I would live. But did I make some unconscious choices?

The milk was still delivered to our door when I was a child in Lexington. We knew the milkman, the paperboy and the mailman, as we do today in our scruffy little village on the edge of the Cotswolds. We knew the neighbours, too, in small-town Kentucky. Who in Lexington now sees their neighbours every day? Our neighbours borrow and return eggs, sugar and milk, as tradition demands. They feed our cats, whose numbers vary from three upwards, when we're away for the night. They take the children for walks and remember their birthdays.

The same person has cleaned our house, ironed our clothes, done the shopping and dealt with the repairmen since we moved to this house fourteen years ago. We expect her to call on us when she or a member of her family is ill, as much as we expect to share her family's occasions for celebration.

Though the house dates from the 1620s, and is older than

anything in Lexington, it is built from similar materials to those found in old Lexington stone houses. So similar is the local Cotswold limestone, that the drystone walls surrounding our garden are identical to those in the rural areas around Lexington. There they are often called 'slave walls', because they are popularly supposed to be of such antiquity that they were built by slave labour. (Perhaps they were: most of the skilled masons around Lexington have continued to be black.) In fact the design of them very obviously migrated from my present home to my former one. But I remember with affectionate amusement the reaction of my then eight-year-old nephew from Lexington, when he saw our Oxfordshire garden drystone walls: 'Did you all have slaves here, too?' The lush greenness of this part of the world is echoed by that of Lexington, and if the sun shone here a bit more often we could grow the flowering dogwood and magnolia I so miss. Roses flourish here, as they did in the garden of the Cooper Road house, the childhood home I loved best.

Perhaps I *have* chosen to go home again, manipulated and manoeuvred the circumstances of life so that my present home across an ocean from my childhood home, nonetheless resembles it in its essentials. Maybe my subconscious has plotted it all, and transported the desirable bits of my old Kentucky home across the sea, where my own children can be brought up with the best of both worlds. It's a sentimental and optimistic view, and makes a virtue of what fate and our own psyches force us to do unthinkingly. It means you can go home again, if only in reverie, and it consoles you that you have cheated your own progeny of nothing. How sad that it is too comfortable to be true.

Afterword

Any reader who has taken the trouble to get this far might like to know where this account of strange childhood, obsessive adolescence and imprudently-spent youth is heading. After no fewer than four universities on both sides of the Atlantic, and one or two changes in the subjects I was studying, I collected some degrees. My research was chiefly to do with the Cambridge philosopher G. E. Moore and the secret society called the Cambridge Apostles. In the course of it I met, and was befriended by, most of the survivors of the Bloomsbury Group, and the legion of workers in the Bloomsbury industry. Michael Holroyd, in particular, was so kind to me that he placed himself in the position of being bound to me by hoops of literary steel, and for many years we have served as joint literary executors of Lytton Strachey.

Harvard, my last university but one, excused me from the requirement of writing a Ph.D. thesis, and offered to take a published book in lieu. They were as good as their word, and when I sent them *G. E. Moore and the Cambridge Apostles* in 1979, they sent me a document in Latin by return of post.

Having got the ultimate qualification to be a university teacher, I immediately gave it up and became a journalist. Since 1974 I had been working on the book pages of the world's oldest Sunday newspaper, the *Observer*, as a reviewer of books about Bloomsbury, art and architecture, sex and any other subject in which I could show a convincing interest. In the meanwhile, I was 'discovered' as a food writer by Ann Barr, the real genius of the magazine *Harper's & Queen*, and worked for her regularly from 1977, almost until we wrote that scurrilously scholarly nice little earner, *The Official Foodie Handbook* in 1984. For by then, I'd become a full-time specialist writer on food and wine, and the staff journalist of the *Observer* who was concerned with those matters. Thousands of articles, and a few books later, I still make most of my bread from food and drink. But Paul Robeson had roles other than Othello, and I do a bit of journalism from time to time (whenever it is offered to me) on other subjects, especially profiles, which I particularly enjoy. And *Moore* is back in print now, just to confound those who think I'm two people with but one name.

The loss of my southern drawl has served me well in my radio and television work where, I'm told, I can almost pass for a native.

It was difficult to detach myself from my perfectly enjoyable daily life to write this book. Time was a problem, but the *Observer* allowed me to take my sabbatical in February and March of 1988. Space was a problem, too. I knew in my bones that I needed to be on neutral ground when I tried to remember what it was like to grow up Jewish in the Bluegrass; I had to be away from my English home and family. Not for the first time, I was gripped by the need to be an alien.

My friend, now Maecenas, Alistair McAlpine understood completely, and offered to lend me a house in the remotest part of the English-speaking world, Broome, in Western Australia. Captain Norman's house was a nineteenth-century pearl-fishing captain's house, one of several Lord McAlpine has rescued and preserved. It stands proud of the earth on inverted chimney-pot-like objects, to avoid the attentions of snakes and nasty insects, and to catch the breeze. This was very necessary. As Alistair had warned, it was frequently 100°F except in the air-conditioned bedroom where I wrote most of the above, and even the inviting swimming pool was the unrefreshing temperature of a warm cup of tea. My wife joined me at the end of my month-long stay. We made an entirely new set of friends and I finished most of this book, living at the other end of the earth, as near the Equator as I could get. It was the next best thing to going to Mars.

Appendix

There is a tradition that my paternal grandmother, Jenny (Yetta or Yachne) Baron Levy's family is related to the family of Rabbi Abraham Isaac Kook (1864–1935, sometimes spelled Kuk when transliterated from Hebrew). I'm confident that this is true, as my grandmother's pantry always contained a little tin charity collection box for the benefit of Rov Kook's yeshiva in Israel, and long after her death my father kept up the family's contribution to this institution. I know, because during my left-wing youth, I strongly disapproved of subsidising what I then thought of as ignorant superstition and religious intolerance, and we sometimes quarrelled about it. In the summer of 1962 my father and I were guests at Rabbi Kook's yeshiva, Merkaz Harav, in Jerusalem. His daughter and the son-in-law who had inherited his Elijah's mantle showed us around the school. I was disturbed at the sight of the very young students, beardless boys, who had given up the secular world for that of a religious learning I could not but despise. We were presented to the assembled boys and youths as founder's kin. They prayed for us in our presence. I had an uncomfortable feeling that, like some Emperor of Japan, they were praying *to* us.

The tradition of the connection with Rabbi Kook is further strengthened by the story of Rabbi Kook's having once come to visit my grandmother in Lexington. I don't actually know their precise degree of relationship. Family members spoke of his having been a 'third cousin'. In strict genealogical terms that would mean that three generations earlier their ancestors had included a pair of siblings. For purposes of constructing a pedigree, however, the exact degree of kinship is not so crucial as the belief that there definitely was a connection. This alone would mean that all Rabbi Kook's ancestors figure in the family tree of Jenny Levy's descendants, for Rabbi Kook and she were nearly contemporary.

Abraham Isaac Kook, the first Chief Rabbi of Palestine under the Mandate, was born in Grieva, Latvia, the son of Shlomo Zalman ha-Cohen. He was rabbi at Zimel and Boisk, and in 1904 rabbi of Jaffa. In 1914 Rabbi Kook was stranded in Europe by the outbreak of the Great War, and in 1916 put his enforced exile to use by becoming rabbi of Machzike Hadath in London. In 1919 he returned to Palestine as rabbi of Jerusalem, and in 1921 became Chief Rabbi of Palestine, which position he occupied until his death on 1 September, 1935.

There are several family stories about Rabbi Kook that are not to be found in print – at least, not in the entries about him in the *Encyclopaedia Britannica* or the *Encyclopædia Judaica*; this lends weight to the supposition that our families are related. One charming anecdote (told me by my great-uncle Nathan, my grandmother's brother) says that during his time as Chief Rabbi he was imprisoned by the British because he was opposed to Partition – or to some aspects of the Partition policy. (This incidentally, explains why there is a Rabbi Kook Street in nearly every Arab village in Israel, and why his memory is revered among Arabs living in Israel: he always favoured a bi-national state.) The British presented for his signature a document conceding at least some of his demands, thinking he was certain to refuse to sign it, as they offered it for his signature on the Sabbath. As a recognised authority on the sacred Law, Rabbi Kook exercised his privilege to change the law concerning Sabbath observance. To the confusion and fury of his captors, he signed. I have been told that the law of Sabbath observance now incorporates Rabbi Kook's amendment. He was a very great theologian; some sources say he was a philosopher, and most agree that he was a bit of a mystic.

His pedigree is well documented; it is one of the chief eastern European lines of rabbinical descent, and is often referred to as 'the unbroken line', for it claims to go back to the Jews of the Bible. Jews of eastern European origin who are trying to trace their own ancestry find time and again that a connection with Rabbi Kook's line yields one of the only traceable pedigrees for Ashkenazi Jews.

Kook was a descendent of Mordecai Jaffe of Prague (1530–1612), the ancestor of a large number of rabbinical families in Italy, Russia, Austria, Germany, the USA and Britain. Mordecai Jaffe's uncle, Moses Jaffe, traced their ancestry to Samuel ben Elhanan, a great-grandson of the sage Rashi (1040–1105). 'Jaffe' is Hebrew for 'beautiful', and the *Jewish Encyclopedia* has no fewer than 132 biographies of various Jaffes. In the archives of the Leo Baeck Institute is a Jaffe family tree beginning in 1650; there are many other sources of records as well. The Jaffe family is related to at least 66 other Jewish families, including the Singers, my mother's family. So far as we know, the name has always been Singer, or one of its cognates in another language, and my brother and I are probably doubly descended from Mordecai Jaffe of Prague.

It is the putative connection of Mordecai Jaffe with Rashi that is the most interesting part of this family tree. Many Ashkenazi rabbinical families claim descent from Rashi both for snobbish reasons (the Jewish notion of aristocracy expressed in the Yiddish word *yichas*), and from much more earth-shattering pretensions. There is a tradition that Rashi, via Hillel the Great (70 BC–10 AD), is directly descended from King David (1043–973 BC). This tradition rests on a pedigree that was patently forged by Jews (though they were no doubt genuine descendants of Rashi) in seventeenth-century Italy. The motive for the forgery is not difficult to imagine: another Jewish tradition is that the Messiah will be descended from the House of David. It was not merely pretending to royal blood that caused His biographers, Matthew and Luke, to construct the identical pedigree for our cousin Jesus of Nazareth.

The Jaffe–Rashi connection can be better grounded. RASHI is an acronym for Rabbi Solomon ben Isaac (Hebrew Reb Shlomo Yitzhaki). In *Finding Our Fathers* (New York, 1977), Dan Rottenberg says of Rashi, 'the revered Talmudic commentator of Troyes, France' that 'several rabbinical families claim descent from him, including Treves, Luria, Katzenellenbogen, Heilprin, Loans and the Zarfati family of Morocco. While their claims are certainly possible, no family can trace its ancestry back to Rashi in an unbroken line.'

I accept that no conclusive documentation exists to relate Mordecai Jaffe to Rashi. But the Jaffe-Rashi connection rests anyway, not on the details of the Rashi family tree, but on accepting the claim of Moses Jaffe, Mordecai's uncle, to be descended from Samuel ben Elhanan. Rashi had three daughters. The eldest, Jochebed, married Meir ben Samuel (1065–1135). They had five children, of whom the youngest, and only daughter, was thought to have been named Miriam. Her issue includes Isaac of Dampierre (obviously still in France; 1120–1195?), who, the dates seem to indicate, was more probably Miriam's grandson than her son. Elhanan (d. 1184) was therefore probably Isaac's son, and Samuel, the ancestor on whose account we are undertaking this exercise, the son of Elhanan, and a great-great-grandson of Rashi. Branches of Rashi's family were still living in France in the sixteenth century, but soon after joined the general eastern Jewish migration.

There is no particular reason to doubt Moses Jaffe's avowal of descent from Samuel ben Elhanan. Its only difficulty is that it is through the female line, whereas all other pretenders to the

Rashi connection (save the cadet branch of Rashi's youngest daughter) have a male, and thus a patronymic, in an earlier generation. The chief reason for any family claiming descent from Rashi is just plain *yichas*: such a connection would be very useful in a rabbinical career.

Rashi himself studied in Worms, returning to Troyes about 1065. The town was then the capital of the Champagne region, and there, supported by the income from the family vineyards, Rashi wrote his famous commentaries. Those on the Old Testament and Talmud rank as the greatest in Jewish exegesis, and are still important in Jewish religious life. His commentary on the Pentateuch was the first dated Hebrew book ever printed (in 1475). Rashi's work influenced the development of Protestantism, as it was known to Luther; it is distinguished by great clarity.

The tradition that Rashi was descended from King David was a strong one, for it gave a kind of unity of rabbinical descent through Hillel, Simeon ha-Nasi, Gamaliel the Elder and the 2nd century AD Johanan ha-Sandalar of Egypt, to Rashi's grandfather, leaving only twenty generations of not very great distinction between ha-Gaon Rabbi Eliakim and Solomon, grandfather of Rashi. This tradition existed well before a seventeenth-century Italian attempted to prove it by faking the documentation. The fact that a fake pedigree exists is, of course, no reason to assume that the tradition itself is false.

Zooming now from the middle ages to the last century, I learnt my grandmother's family history from a kinsman I've never met, David Nurco, an academic living in Baltimore, Maryland, who had the clever idea of doing a one-day census of the descendants of the family living in the United States in 1976.

Dr Nurco has traced the family back to four brothers named Baron, born in Kavarsk, Lithuania, one of whom was my great-grandfather. (The spelling of the name, transliterated from the Russian, Yiddish, German or Hebrew original has one 'r', according to branches of the family in Manhattan and Westchester County, and two according to those in Louisville and Lexington, Kentucky, Cincinnati, Ohio and in Los Angeles, where, in 1976, cousin Bernard Barron was Vice President of 20th Century Fox, no less.)

The father of the Baron brothers was, says Dr Nurco, 'apparently in charge of a business which produced pottery used for cooking utensils that were sold to the farmers in the surrounding countryside . . . The eldest brother, Naftola, left Kavarsk and married Yetta. Family history places them in Raguva, Kovono Gubernija, Lithuania; however, some early documents in the United States state that at least one of his children was born in Riga, Latvia.' 'Kovono Gubernija' is one of the place names I can recall being mentioned in my childhood. 'Kovno' is the Russian for Kaunas, the second town of Lithuania, an important commercial centre even in mediaeval times.

Naftola Baron studied at a yeshiva, but failed to become a rabbi. His in-laws owned a flour mill, but proved inept at business, and family lore says he would cross the road to avoid embarrassing those who owed him money. He and Yetta had five children. He emigrated to New York, followed shortly by his eldest daughter. His wife and remaining children only came to the Williamsbridge area of New York after his death.

The other brothers all spent their lives in Europe, but several of their children emigrated to America and settled in Lexington and Cincinnati. They adopted the surnames Gordon, Berkowitz and Herman. Berkowitz is the easiest to explain: to avoid conscription, one of the original four brothers, Avram Dov, was legally adopted by a family called Berkowitz. As their 'only son', he was exempt from military service, and allowed to continue his yeshiva studies.

My ancestor was the second son, Yechiel Asher Baron, 'a scholarly and religious man', says Dr Nurco, who was a Hebrew teacher and ran a *cheder* or religious school. In Kavarsk he had educated both his daughters, Jenny (or Yachne) and my great-aunt Ethel, as well as his sons, Sam, Ben and Nathan, all three of whom went to yeshivoth. My grandmother was so clever that she became an assistant to her father. Sam became a *shochet*, a ritual slaughterer. Ben was a prodigy at his Talmudic studies, and was teaching other children by the age of ten.

Though I don't remember Sam, the others I knew quite well. There is a splendid photograph of all of them except Sam (but including Grandfather Levy), taken some time in the early 1950s, sent me by one of my favourite, if distant, cousins. (She is a first cousin, once removed. But our clan's network is such, that we keep in touch, not only with her and her husband, but with one of their sons.) She says, with justice, that in it Joe Levy looks straight out of a William Faulkner novel – in Yiddish, and asks if I 'remember Aunt Ethel? A sweet, defeated and oppressed woman'. I certainly do. She was deaf, and her accented English was strange, compounded as it was of Yiddish, a regional American drawl and the peculiar speech difficulties of the deaf. My cousin's father Nathan, my favourite of that generation, looks amiable and amused, while his brother Ben looks worn out. My grandmother is sporting a large orchid corsage – could the occasion have been their 50th wedding anniversary?

To return to the parents of that generation, the third Baron brother, Chona, says Dr Nurco, was described 'as a good-hearted, pleasant man with a wonderful sense of humour. Though he was poor and made his living with a horse and wagon he often sang, even when he was hungry. His wife was a religious woman with gentle respect for all life. She would collect clothing, money and food for those poorer than her own family.'

Finally the youngest and most interesting brother, Avram Dov Berkowitz. He was so musical that he sang at weddings aged three, and he naturally became a cantor as well as a rabbi when he attended the Valkamir yeshiva, in Lithuania, where he was a close friend of the Hebrew poet Yehoash (Solomon Bloomgarden or Blumengarten, 1870–1927, emigrated to America in 1891), whose greatest achievement was to translate the Hebrew Scriptures into vernacular Yiddish. Avram Dov was taught Hebrew by Moses Leib Lilienblum, an early Zionist. He played the violin and was the composer of some original liturgical melodies. He spent four years in Johannesburg, South Africa, where he was shochet as well as rabbi and cantor. He educated his daughters as well as his sons. In 1914 when war broke out, Avram Dov and his family were evacuated from Lithuania to a Jewish colony in Ekaterinoslav (now Dnepropetrovsk), in the Ukraine, where he again worked as rabbi and cantor; he was killed along with other Jews of that settlement in a pogrom in 1918. His wife and two younger children escaped and joined the four older children in America. The eldest daughter, incidentally, was Sara Goller, which explains my grandmother's connection with her funeral orator, Harry Goller. He was the husband of my grandmother's first cousin.

It occurs to me to wonder that the father of the four Baron brothers of Kavarsk, Lithuania, should have been so humble a man. We don't even know his name, and he appears to have been either an artisan or a very small businessman. Yet only a few hundred miles away in Latvia he had some very well-born cousins. But on reflection I think this is not so remarkable. We are accustomed to thinking of the immigration of Jews to America as a story of unimpeded progress from the *shtetlach* to real civilisation and prosperity, and to congratulating ourselves and our immediate forebears on their rise from poverty and on their relentless upwards social mobility.

The history of my family appears, though, to tell quite another story: one of downward social mobility, coupled, sometimes, with improving economic circumstances. The family of Rabbi Kook held their own socially and financially, and preserved their aristocratic traditions, while relatives only a small distance away were in poverty. What probably had happened is that the parents and grandparents of Jenny Baron Levy had come down in worldly terms, while their Cohen Kook relatives continued to flourish. The present generation of my father's family is distantly aware of its connection with the Kook family, though unconcerned with or ignorant of the joint pedigree. Socially and economically, I reckon the families cannot have diverged much earlier than three generations before Grandmother Levy. Of course, one is calculating Kook's own educational achievements in secular terms, and this might be quite wrong. His only secular accomplishments may well have been the several languages which, after all, any well-travelled Jew of the time would have spoken if not read.

Above all, though, we must not overlook the possibility, even likelihood, that the Kook connection does not go through the Baron line at all, but through Grandmother Levy's mother, the unnamed wife of Yechiel Asher Baron. This might explain why, though the Kooks are Cohens, or descendants of the priestly caste who had special rights and duties in the synagogue, none of the three sons of Yechiel, each of whom went to a yeshiva, ever claimed to be Cohens themselves. This might also explain why the female children of Yechiel Asher were educated, against all custom and expectation – viz., that the tradition stemmed from their mother's family. If so, this heritage of female intellectual prowess and leadership was certainly kept alive by my grandmother.